PRAISE FOR
UNLE~~ASH THE POWER~~
OF ~~S~~

"When a book is title~~d~~ _~~g~~_, you expect it to... well, tell ~~~~ ~~~~ ~~~~ engaging, no-nonsense, and often extremely funny handbook on the craft behind great stories, Rob Biesenbach does indeed tell you stories ... and does so masterfully. He shares his own storytelling roadmap without hesitation, giving you precisely what you need to raise your business storytelling to an art form. Take a bow, Rob, because this one gets a standing ovation from me!"
Shonali Burke, ABC, President & CEO,
Shonali Burke Consulting

"There is no greater skill that will positively impact your career as much as becoming a masterful storyteller. Well-told stories have the power to teach, clarify, and inspire. Rob's experience and unique point of view makes him a go-to authority for ambitious leaders. I have enjoyed all of Rob's books and _Unleash the Power of Storytelling_ is no exception."
Patricia Fripp, Past President,
National Speakers Association

"Storytelling is hard; just ask Ernest Hemingway. Rob Biesenbach makes it as easy as possible for you to become the Hemingway of your organization. In this book he reveals the secrets of good storytelling to help you create stories that command attention in this distracted age."
Dr. Nick Morgan, Communications Coach and Author
of _Power Cues_ and _Give Your Speech, Change the World_

"Rob Biesenbach's terrific book, *Unleash The Power of Storytelling*, is true to its claim that it's a practical guide for the workplace, the marketplace, and everyday life. It offers storytelling tips from cradle to grave, from how to craft a memorable origin story for a company to creating a heartfelt eulogy for a loved one. His parting words, 'Most of all, don't hold back. Don't let fear override your desire to share. Be open and generous and allow your individuality to shine through,' is great advice for storytelling and life."
Patrice Tanaka, Public Speaker, Founder & Chief Joy Officer, Joyful Planet LLC

"All the experts suggest you tell stories — in content, in speeches, in sales, in customer experience, in every aspect of business. But no one tells you how. That's where *Unleash the Power of Storytelling* comes in. Rob Biesenbach provides a five-step process for crafting your stories, and six ways to ensure they're relevant to your audience. After you read this book, you'll never again have to wonder … 'but how?'"
Gini Dietrich, Founder and Author, *Spin Sucks*

UNLEASH THE
POWER OF
STORYTELLING

WIN HEARTS, CHANGE MINDS,
GET RESULTS

UNLEASH THE POWER OF STORYTELLING

WIN HEARTS, CHANGE MINDS, GET RESULTS

ROB BIESENBACH

Eastlawn Media

To Teddy and Lily:
I can't wait to watch your stories unfold.

Unleash the Power of Storytelling:
Win Hearts, Change Minds, Get Results

Copyright © 2018 Rob Biesenbach

Published by Eastlawn Media
2011 Orrington Ave Evanston, IL 60201

ISBN: 978-0-9910814-2-4

CONTENTS

PART TWO: ADVANCED STORYTELLING

PART THREE: APPLIED STORYTELLING

INTRODUCTION:
WHY STORYTELLING IS ESSENTIAL TO SUCCESS

I do an exercise in my workshops where I have audience members craft a short story and pair up with others to tell it. Most people take to the activity right away, and the room brims with energy as people discover the wealth of stories that reside within them.

But a few people get stumped. Like the nice woman in Ballroom B a couple of years ago whose expression was as blank as the sheet of paper in front of her.

I came down from the stage and offered to help. "I just can't think of a story," she said.

"What do you do?" I asked.

"I'm in IT."

"Okay, what's the biggest challenge you face?"

"Oh, that's easy. People ignore all our procedures and warnings and end up downloading viruses and malware."

"So do you have an example of someone who did something stupid that infected your systems and caused chaos?"

"Of course!" she said.

"That's your story."

Stories are all around us. We may not recognize them, but they're there — just waiting to be found, shaped, and shared.

And when we tap into the power of stories, we can sway opinion, influence people to act and even stop them from doing stupid things — in a way that's far more effective than a list of "dos and don'ts."

Storytelling is arguably the most powerful form of communication at our disposal. More than facts and data and other bits of information, stories are fundamental to persuasion.

It's a Noisy World

There's a lot of confusion out there about storytelling.

And it's not for lack of information. Two years ago I wrote that if you Google the term "storytelling in business" you'll get more than 17 million search results. As of this writing, I got more than *48 million* hits.

There's no doubt that corporate storytelling is a big business these days, with endless articles, research, studies, books, workshops, experts, and other sources of information.

One of those experts, author and professor Jennifer Aaker, compares storytelling to the signal that stands out amidst the noise.[1] That is, in an age of information overload, stories manage to cut through the clutter, offering meaning and significance.

I think this analogy works just as well for the study of storytelling itself. Because there's a lot of noise out there about storytelling and not a lot of signal. A lot of hype, and not much clarity.

Even about the basic things like, "What is a story?" and how do you go about finding, shaping, and telling a good story?

Does Storytelling Intimidate You?

I find there are two kinds of people when it comes to storytelling.

First, there are those who are completely confused and intimidated. Like our IT manager, they may think their everyday experiences offer inadequate fodder for stories worth sharing. But once you become attuned to stories, you'll find no shortage of material.

Or they think storytelling is for the experts — songwriters, poets, the kind of people whose every word keeps you on the edge of your seat.

Part of the problem is TED Talks. We watch these master storytellers reduce their audiences to tears or send them into fits of laughter. But not every story has to pack that kind of punch.

Sometimes it's enough to provoke a simple nod or smile — an acknowledgment of a shared experience or a universal truth.

So if you think you lack the skills or life experiences to tell a good story, let me assure you that storytelling is not as hard as you think. I believe that with the right structure and process, anyone can learn to tell a good story.

Or Are You Overconfident?

At the opposite end of the spectrum, and far more problematic, are the self-proclaimed natural born storytellers. As far as they're concerned, there's nothing about storytelling that they don't already know. To them I would say, "Are you sure? It actually may be more complicated than you think."

Because a lot of things get passed off as stories these days that are not actually stories. An inspirational quote from Steve Jobs or Mahatma Gandhi, for instance, is not a story. (Even when it's superimposed over an image of a pretty sunset!)

A customer testimonial in and of itself is not necessarily a story. A fact sheet is certainly not a story. Most case studies I've read are barely stories.

Stories — *real* stories — contain certain fundamental, timeless elements that give them their power. Ignore those fundamentals at your peril. You could end up squandering an opportunity to change minds and even lives.

Clarifying and Demystifying Storytelling

So whether you underestimate or overestimate your storytelling abilities, this book offers plenty for you to learn. It's designed to clarify and demystify the storytelling process and to give you practical tools you can use right away to become a better storyteller.

Among the lessons covered:

- We'll talk about what makes stories so powerful. Storytelling is not a soft skill — there is actual hard science behind it. And I believe the more you know about *why* stories work, the better you'll be able to *make* your stories work.

- I'll offer a simple structure that can be used to craft practically any story.

- You'll see examples of lots of different kinds of stories. Stories that are targeted to different audiences (customers, employees, the public) and told through different channels, from spoken word to digital to video.

- I'll show you how to declutter your stories — ridding them of the extraneous details that bog down so many stories.

- You'll learn a process for uncovering good stories and bringing out the best stories in others.

- We'll look at some of the pitfalls of storytelling and how to avoid them.

- And in the final section we'll explore how you can use stories in a variety of situations, from formal presentations to job interviews to wedding toasts.

What Stories Can Do for You

By the end of the book, you'll come away with the mindset and roadmaps necessary to tell better stories, which can help you in multiple ways in the workplace, in the marketplace, and in your everyday life.

A great story can help you:

- Win hearts — captivating, inspiring and motivating an audience.

- Change minds — convincing people to come around to your way of thinking.

- Get results — persuading them to act in a way that helps you achieve your goals.

That means the ability to better:

- Market your business

- Promote your brand

- Close a sale

- Attract investors

- Strengthen relationships with customers

- Build trust with employees

- Rally a team

- Align people with a strategy

- Attract the best and brightest talent

- Win over a skeptic

- Become a more comfortable networker

- Nail a job interview

- Earn a raise

- Give a toast

- Deliver a eulogy

- Get out of a speeding ticket

- And much, much more …

A Practical Guide for the Busy Professional

I try to write the kind of business books I would want to read. That means practical, succinct, and entertaining.

If you lean toward the theoretical or philosophical, this is not the book for you. Most of these lessons are drawn from actual experience consulting with clients, teaching workshops, writing for the stage, and performing in front of audiences.

But if you want a straightforward, hands-on guide that will load you up with tons of tips on storytelling … if you want lessons you can use right away to become a more effective storyteller and communicator … and if you think a book about storytelling ought to be filled with good stories … then keep reading.

Drawing From the World of Performance

About that "performing" thing. Here is my story, and what it means for your reading experience:

In the early 2000s I started a second career as an actor. By day I was serving my business clients and by night I was auditioning, rehearsing, and performing.

For the longest time I kept these worlds separate, thinking they had nothing to do with each other. But the more I studied and performed, the more I realized that the worlds of business and acting were not so different.

They both require you to connect with an audience, to express yourself creatively and, most of all, to tell stories. As I often tell my clients, if you want to stand out, if you want to be creative, stop looking at what other businesses are doing, and start looking at show business.

This is the basis of my books and workshops. I believe every communication presents an opportunity — and an obligation — to perform. And if you apply the proven techniques that actors use to make the most of that performance, you're going to be a more successful communicator.

Workshop audiences find this approach fun and relatable, and I think it makes for an entertaining read as well.

PART ONE:
STORYTELLING ESSENTIALS

CHAPTER 1:
WHAT MAKES STORIES SO POWERFUL?

Study after study confirms what we all know intuitively: stories are uniquely powerful.

We witness that power when we dry our tears as the house lights come up. When the book we put down sticks with us for days, months, and years. And when we hold our loved ones a little closer after watching a tragic tale play out on the news.

If you want to break down walls with people, truly connect with them, and make an impact, few things beat a well-crafted, well-told story.

There is both a nature and a nurture argument behind why stories are so effective. Let's start with nurture.

We are Raised on Stories

Bedtime stories, fables, fairy tales, cartoons — we are immersed in stories from nearly the moment we're born. And we're inundated with them throughout our lives.

Worldwide we spend $90 billion a year on movies and another $90 billion on video games. And we watch more than 30 hours a week of television (at least in the United States, which appears to lead the world in this dubious distinction).[2]

So stories are embedded in our consciousness. When someone says they're going to tell us a story, it sets certain expectations in our mind. We assume it will follow a familiar pattern — setup, climax, resolution. When it doesn't, we are left dissatisfied.

As Kendall Haven argues in his book *Story Proof*, "The steady diet of stories that children experience modifies the brain to render it more predisposed to think in story terms."[3]

And that's where things get really interesting.

Our Brains are Hardwired for Stories

Multiple studies show that stories have a unique effect on our brains.[4] Researcher Paul Zak found that stories cause the brain to produce oxytocin, a chemical related to feelings of empathy and a desire to cooperate.[5] This essentially softens up our audience, making them more amenable to our ideas.

Stories stimulate our senses in multiple ways, to the extent that listening goes from being a passive exercise to an active experience. In fact, multiple studies have shown that when we hear a story, it triggers the same areas of the brain that are stimulated when we experience an event.[6]

Think about that for a moment: as far as the brain is concerned, there's little distinction between story and experience.

And this is what makes stories so powerful: they sweep us up and involve us in multiple important ways — physiologically, emotionally, intellectually:

- As storytelling expert Nancy Duarte describes in a popular TED Talk, great stories cause our palms to sweat, our hearts to race, our eyes to dilate.[7]

- Emotionally, we empathize with the protagonist, we identify with her struggle.

- Mentally, we put ourselves inside that story, asking the essential questions, "What would I do in these circumstances? How would I measure up?"

Stories Trump Statistics

In the influential book *Made to Stick*, one of the authors did a memory exercise with his university students in which they listened to a series of presentations and were tested on what they retained.[8] He found that while 63 percent remembered the stories they heard, just 5 percent could recall the statistics presented.

Stories stick. Here's one that stuck with me.

I was working with a company that makes candy and gum, and they wanted to demonstrate their commitment to quality. So we put together a video crew and went looking for stories.

That's when I met Estela, a factory worker whose job was to inspect packages of gum before they left the plant. I asked her what she does to ensure quality in her work.

Not surprisingly, my process-oriented question got a process-oriented answer. She walked me through her routines from the start of the line to the finish. She showed me the x-ray machine that checks for bits of metal, and she pointed to a laminated sheet with a matrix of various quality criteria that she judges each pack of gum on.

For many companies, this would be their story:

> *Our people are passionately committed to quality. They're on the line every day, utilizing state-of-the-art technology to test for impurities and applying our strict 24-point quality checklist, all to ensure that the gum you're enjoying right now is as fresh and tasty as the day it left our door!*

But that's not a story; it's just a bunch of facts, claims, and data. And those don't stick.

Get to the Heart of It

I then went to the figurative heart of the matter. I knew Estela had children, so I asked her what they think about what she does. That's when she lit up. "They call me the Candy Lady," she beamed.

Then she turned over one of the packages of gum and showed me a code on the bottom. That code tells you exactly when and where the gum was made, right down to the individual shift and production line.

And here's the kicker: her children can read the code. So what do you think happens when her family goes to the store? The kids run straight to the candy aisle, turn over the packages of gum, and when they find the right code, they yell out, "This is Mommy's gum! Mommy made this gum."

Now *that's* a story. Here's a company you can count on for quality. It's good enough for your family because Estela is down there on the line every day making sure it's good enough for hers.

Six Keys to Powerful Stories

Estela's story perfectly illustrates six key ingredients that give stories their power.

1. **Stories tap into emotion**
   The best stories trigger an emotional response, which is key to provoking empathy in our audience and unlocking decision-making. Research suggests that "emotionally charged events" carry far more weight and persistence in our memory than ordinary, neutral events.[9] (For more on the role of emotion, see Chapter 4.)

2. **Stories put a face on an issue**
   In the end, nobody cares about processes or programs; they care about people. So if you can embody your idea, your initiative, your brand in a great character that people can relate to, you're going to have more success.

3. **Stories connect us**
   Most people have never stepped foot in a candy factory, but they can still identify with Estela's story. Why? Because it's not about candy manufacturing; it's about a mom looking out for the health and well-being of her children — something most of us can relate to.

4. **Stories humanize us**
   The stories we tell offer a glimpse into who we are and what we value. And that's highly appealing. It's especially important for leaders — people want to follow humans, not machines.

5. **They raise the stakes**
   The Estela story is not about manufacturing standards or error rates. It's about health and safety and love and family. Stories raise us up out of the everyday and the mundane, appealing instead to universal values that bring us all together.

6. **Stories are about "show, don't tell"**
   As one of my instructors put it, "Actors express themselves through actions. That's why they're called actors, not talkers." It's better to *show* us who you are and what you stand for than to just *tell* us about it. And that's one of the things stories do best.

Defeating Match.com Syndrome

The principle of "show, don't tell" is the antidote to something I call "match.com syndrome." If you spend time on any dating site you'll find that everyone describes themselves the same way. They say they're "funny, intelligent, and adventurous." (Would that that were true!)

These kinds of generic claims are ineffective because everyone makes them. Plus, few of us are objective judges of our own stellar qualities.

But "show, don't tell" means that instead of *saying* you're funny, *be* funny. Instead of *saying* you're intelligent, *talk about* the last book you read. Instead of *saying* you're adventurous, *post a picture* of that white-water rafting trip you took.

All of those things together are going to paint a much more compelling and credible picture of who you are than any of the common labels we apply to ourselves.

Which we do all the time, as individuals and as organizations. "I'm resourceful," "I'm reliable," "I'm creative." Or, "We offer personal attention," "We provide the highest quality," "We care."

Stories give proof to these claims and they set us apart. Because anyone can talk about service excellence, but nobody else has your particular story about the overjoyed customer and the employee who bent over backward to personally resolve her issue.

A Lesson From *The Godfather*

This discussion leads us to *The Godfather* films, which any fan will tell you offer lessons for practically every circumstance in life.

In the opening scene of the first film we instantly recognize that Don Vito Corleone is a man to be reckoned with. Dressed in a tuxedo, he sits stoically in a darkened room behind a big desk, patiently listening to a nervous man pleading for his help.

It's all right there in the story: show, don't tell.

Now what if the movie opened with the Don saying, "Welcome to my office. I'm the most powerful leader of the five families. How can I use my vast criminal empire to crush your enemies today?"

That wouldn't be particularly effective (or entertaining).

Always challenge yourself to dispense with the hollow claims and tell stories instead:

- On your website, don't just say your people provide "hands-on" attention, tell us about the senior VP rolling up his sleeves and working away with the rest of the team.

- During a sales pitch, don't just talk about quality, tell us about the customer who gave you that five-star review.

- In a job interview, don't just say you're dependable, tell us how you worked all night to meet an impossible deadline.

Whether you're selling, interviewing, or just representing yourself in the marketplace, offer people something they can't refuse: a specific story that lends power to your words.

CHAPTER 2:
WHAT IS A STORY?

When I ask workshop audiences to define story for me, I get as many answers as there are people in the room.

Some say a story is a journey or an experience or a happening. Others say a story is about conflict, or that a story has a beginning, a middle, and an end.

That last one is my personal favorite, and it appears frequently in how-to articles on storytelling. Yes, stories must have a beginning, a middle, and an end — but there's a lot more to it than that.

For instance, if I wanted to get to Carnegie Hall (I know, practice!) and I entered the destination into my navigation app, it wouldn't be all that helpful if the directions said:

- In the beginning, leave your garage

- In the middle, drive 806 miles

- In the end, arrive at 881 7th Avenue, New York

So how do you get you from point A to point B? You need a structure.

A Simple Structure for Telling Any Story

A colleague was writing a book on storytelling and his research turned up 82 different definitions of story. (Which goes to show you, there really are no wrong answers to the question, "What is a story?")

After all that work, the definition he settled on was similar to the one I learned at Chicago's famed Second City, the birthplace of comic legends from Joan Rivers to John Belushi to Tina Fey.

(And, no, Tina and I did not share a stage. I was one of thousands of ordinary people enrolled at its training center to study the art of improvisational and sketch comedy.)

In its simplest form, a story is a **character** in pursuit of a **goal** in the face of some **challenge** or obstacle.

How the character tries to **resolve** that challenge drives the narrative. Now you could argue that "resolution" is a fourth element to story structure, but I think that's implicit. After all, if you're talking about overcoming a challenge to achieve a goal, it has to resolve in some way.

Now there are undoubtedly other elements to story — a turning point, climax, denouement, and more — but character, goal, and challenge are the three legs of the stool. Without these three, you don't have a story.

Plus, three is just an easier number to manage. An audience member once told me he went to a seminar that taught eight ingredients for storytelling — he said he couldn't remember any of them but was pretty sure he could nail these three.

Story Structure at Work

Since people innately respond to stories (whether they can define them or not), getting the structure right is essential to success. So let's look at a few examples to help bring these principles to life:

- In the story I told in the previous chapter about the candy factory, our **character** is Estela and her **goal** is to turn out a quality product. The **challenge** she faces is how to maintain her focus on quality in the face of such a repetitive (some might say boring) task — watching packages of gum go by all day. Estela **resolves** that challenge by thinking of her customers as being as important to her as her own children.

- In *Romeo and Juliet*, our **characters** are two naïve young lovers. Their **goal** is to be together, and the **challenge** they face is the blood feud that divides their families. Whether they **resolve** this challenge is up to you and your own beliefs. They do end up together, right? In death, if not the afterlife. Beware of what you wish for!

- In the TV classic "I Love Lucy," our **character** is Lucy Ricardo, the zany redhead living in New York with her bandleader husband. The **goal** driving much of her action is to get into show business, and her **challenges** are many: her husband Ricky won't put her in his show, she's not particularly talented, and she becomes her own worst enemy through her outlandish attempts to win a part. As for the **resolution**, therein lies the legendary "high jinks" central to this and any sitcom.

For your homework, try casting a more analytical eye on the TV and movies you watch. You're sure to find this structure everywhere, and if you work with it enough, it will eventually become second nature — you'll be using it to frame your stories without even knowing it.

How to Bullet-proof Your Structure

Those are the fundamental elements of story structure. Put them together and you have a pretty reliable foundation for your story to stand on.

But even with those elements, your story may come up short, failing to grip the audience in the way you intend.

If your story feels flat and you can't identify the problem, give special attention to these five issues.

1. IS THE CHARACTER REAL AND RELATABLE?

Your character must be a specific individual. This is the problem with the typical dry corporate case study. It's written from 30,000 feet — from an institutional perspective.

Bring your stories down to the human level. If a problem exists it must surely affect actual people!

And the character must be relatable to the audience — close to them in circumstances, values, or other qualities. (More on character in the next chapter.)

2. IS THERE SUFFICIENT CONFLICT?

Without conflict you have no drama. Conflict arises from the tension between the character's goal and the challenge facing her.

Nobody wants to read a story that goes like this:

> *Our client was having a systems integration issue. We put together a crack team of experts who applied their know-how and resolved the problem to the client's delight.*

When everything goes well or as planned, there's no drama to hold the audience's attention. We need to hear more about the client's struggles — how they tried different approaches but were thwarted.

Or perhaps there was a hitch in the plan — a problem the team hadn't encountered before or a hurdle they weren't sure they could overcome.

If your story doesn't have strong conflict, it's not a story. Keep digging.

3. ARE THE STAKES HIGH ENOUGH?

For a story to work, there has to be something important at stake — a serious problem that cries out for action.

There's a big difference between an issue that causes your character a minor inconvenience and one that costs tens of millions of dollars. Go big with your stories.

4. IS THERE CLEAR CAUSE AND EFFECT?

Causality is an important principle in storytelling. It means events are connected to each other in a cause-and-effect relationship — "this happened, so that happened," or "this happened, but that happened."[10]

Causality is more meaningful to us than mere coincidence.

A sure sign of a weak story is when you find yourself saying "and then" over and over again. "This happened, and then that happened, and then she said, and then he said," etc.

Make sure to tightly link the chain of events in your story.

5. IS THERE AN EMOTIONAL CORE?

Emotion fuels stories. When your audience *feels* something, they are more likely to *do* something (to act in the way you want them to act — buy, get on board, change their behavior, etc.).[11]

So your story must provoke an emotional response that your audience can relate to — the frustration over long waiting times, the disappointment of a blown opportunity, the joy of victory.

We'll explore the importance of emotion in Chapter 4.

About that Beginning, Middle, and End

Getting back to the "beginning, middle, and end": here is how our structure aligns with each of those phases.

In the **beginning**, you set the scene and introduce the **character**:

It was just another Saturday night for Sheila, a budding entrepreneur with her own growing fashion line. She was enjoying catching up with friends over dinner.

This brings the listener into the world you're introducing. It's the "normal" state. Next, something happens that upsets the balance:

Suddenly an alert popped up on her phone. It was a message from her biggest customer: THE SHIPMENT NEVER ARRIVED!

That's the inciting incident (or **challenge**) that sets the story in motion.

The **middle** is where the character works to overcome the challenge, trying to restore balance to the world — in this case, fulfilling the order and winning back the customer's confidence (the **goal**):

She rushed back to the office, searching through tracking numbers and desperately trying to get in touch with someone at the shipping company. Then she discovered the problem: beneath a pile of inventory was the box containing the customer's order — packed, labeled and ready to go. She forgot to send it!

The **end** is where things come to a **resolution**:

She checked the clock: 11 pm — too late to ship the package. Her customer needed it for his 10 am store opening. She grabbed the box, ran downstairs, and hailed a cab to the airport. She got a ticket on the redeye to New York and was able to personally deliver the order to her relieved customer just before his store opened.

The normal state is restored — the customer gets his delivery. The moral of this story might be that fanatical commitment to customer service saves the day. Or perhaps the story goes in another direction. The normal state is not restored and the character is forced to make a change, to find a "new normal":

> *The customer got his order, but was still angry about the mix-up and ended the relationship. Sheila lost the customer, a night of sleep, a day away from her business, and hundreds of dollars in airfare. That's when she realized the operation was getting too big to run on her own. She decided it was time to hire full-time help.*

Not all stories have happy endings. Sometimes the resolution is not about getting what you want, but what you need.

There is No One Best Way to Structure a Story

As I said, there are lots of different ways to structure a story beyond character, goal, and challenge. In fact, I just outlined one of those ways (and will return to it in Chapter 13): normal state, inciting incident, turning point, conflict, resolution.

So don't feel bound by the structure I use. It's one that I've found useful, and many of my clients have as well. But everyone's different. Maybe you're the 10- or 15-part type. That's one of the beauties of storytelling — it's as much an art as it is a science.

But let's move on to the next phase: taking these parts and pieces and assembling them into a coherent whole.

CHAPTER 3:
HOW TO CREATE A STORY

Just as there are many ways to define and structure a story, there are countless approaches to creating a story. This is not like building a house, where the foundation must be laid before the walls are constructed and the walls must go up before the roof is added.

Storytelling can be approached from multiple angles. Maybe you've got a particular problem you want to illustrate, or a specific goal in mind. Perhaps you come across an irresistible character who's a veritable fount of great stories.

If you're very lucky, a story will just land in your lap *and* it will come at just the right time when you need it. More often than not, you'll have to find and create one.

So even though this is not an exact science, let me offer a few approaches that might be helpful.

In a Nutshell: Creating Your Story

Creating a story involves these basic steps:

1. Determine who you are trying to reach (your **audience**) and find out as much as you can about them.

2. Figure out what you want them to do — buy your product, work more efficiently, follow you into proverbial battle. That's the **goal**.

3. Think through the **challenges** that may get in the way of that goal — lack of budget, outdated technology, distrust.

4. Find a **character** who has overcome that challenge — by appealing to value over price, working around technology, discovering common ground.

5. Make sure there's a **resolution** to your story.

This does not have to be a sequential process. For instance, it's unlikely that you will simply dream up an audience you want to reach without having an idea of what you want them to do. That is, you might want:

- A customer to buy from you

- An employee to work more efficiently

- The public to trust you

But for the sake of this exercise, let's break these down separately and in order.

1. Identify and Understand Your Audience

Knowing your audience is the first rule of show business, and it's the biggest issue in putting together a story that truly connects with people. So find out as much as you can about them.

The first (and obvious) step is to identify who they are.

Broadly, your audience may be:

- Customers

- Employees

- Suppliers

- Members

- Volunteers

- Donors

- The public

- Shareholders

- Competitors

- An adversary

- Your leadership

- A potential employer

- A potential recruit

- A board of directors

- A jury

- And so on …

Now you want to make sure you really understand them. Here are some questions to ask yourself.

WHO ARE THEY?

Don't rely on assumptions about your audience: do your research. If it's a big group, like customers or employees, look at product or service reviews, focus group findings, survey data, and other sources. Talk to people close to the audience or reach out to representative members of the group.

If it's an individual or small group, check out their online profiles.

Here's the tricky part. Even if it's an audience you already know, *don't skip this phase*. Familiarity breeds complacency. Think hard about who they *really* are. What are their needs, interests, and emotional hot buttons?

WHAT DO THEY WANT?

It's not enough for you to understand your own goal; you have to understand what your audience wants, too. Because if your story doesn't address their needs and interests, it's not going to resonate with them.

People want different things at different times — and often at the same time! Does your audience want something explicit like:

- A lower price?
- A better deal?
- A raise?
- Recognition?
- Clear direction?

And implicitly, do they want:

- Security?

- A feeling of winning?

- A sense of belonging?

- To feel proud?

- Hope in the future?

WHAT DO YOU HAVE IN COMMON?

Here you need to find a bridge between your goal and their needs and desires. What is it that brings you together? For instance:

- Management and employees share a sense of pride in a company's heritage or a love of its products.

- A nonprofit and its volunteers both want to make the world a better place.

- Potential customers presumably feel the same frustration over an unsolved problem that led an entrepreneur to start his business.

On a simpler level, you and your audience may share a love of children or wine or football. A story on one of those subjects can break the ice and create some affinity.

WHAT ARE THEIR DOUBTS, FEARS, AND MISPERCEPTIONS?

Just as important as understanding what brings us together is knowing what drives us apart. Smart storytellers will have a good read on their audience's doubts, fears, and misperceptions — about them, their ideas, and who or what they represent.

Maybe your audience thinks you're inexperienced, or an outsider, or lacking certain skills. A story can be an incredibly effective tool for acknowledging the elephant in the room. It shows humility and self-awareness, disarms skeptics, and can be a starting point for a relationship.

Or if the assumptions about you are mistaken, the right story can help you knock down people's objections.

WHAT DO THEY KNOW?

We move through different circles throughout the day. We communicate with family, colleagues, customers, vendors, neighbors, strangers — each of whom knows us a little differently.

So a story we tell a customer may require more background or setup than one we tell a close friend. Likewise, a story we share with co-workers may need to be simplified and stripped of jargon when shared with people outside the organization.

This can be a serious challenge for people who are steeped in deep technical knowledge. It's easy to forget that outsiders don't speak the language you take for granted. So always ask yourself what's going to be most meaningful to your audience. Should you use the term "ISO 9000" or simply say "quality control system?"

WHAT IS THEIR MOOD, MINDSET, AND CULTURE?

Finally, you need to get a sense of what's really going on in your audience's world. You don't want to tell a funny story about getting fired to a group that's just gone through a round of layoffs.

Find out as much as you can about your audience. Ask:

- What are their sensitivities?

- Are there any hot buttons to avoid?

- Are there any big events going on in their lives that you should know about?

- What about the culture? Is it formal or laid back? Conservative or edgy?

That's the advance work. You also need to maintain a constant state of awareness during the actual process of telling the story. Read the room. What's the mood? Are people agitated? Impatient? Frustrated?

Be prepared to adjust the tone and content of your story or even ditch it entirely if you sense a "bad vibe" or if there are too many unknowns. Always be calculating the potential risks and rewards.

Now that we've covered audience considerations, let's move on to the other four steps.

2. Determine Your Goal

The goal of your story might be immediate and concrete: you want your audience to buy or change their behavior or get on board with their support.

With the Estela story from Chapter 1, our goal was to get all the employees in the organization to understand that quality is their job. It doesn't matter if they're on the front line or in the back office — everyone is responsible for quality.

But sometimes the goal is "softer." You just want to break the ice, give people a glimpse of who you are and what you value, or lay the groundwork for a relationship.

Starting with the goal is the best and most strategic way to begin creating a story. After that, it gets trickier.

3. Discover the Challenge(s)

Logically it may make sense to start mapping out the obstacles standing in the way of your story's goal — insufficient training, lack of teamwork, inadequate systems ...

But in the real world, those challenges are often discovered along the way as you do your research with your story's characters. This is how Estela's story unfolded. We interviewed lots of different employees about how they go about ensuring quality (our goal). Through that process, we uncovered a host of challenges — boredom, technology, supply issues, shift changes, etc.

We also discovered a number of resolutions — how they solved those problems — which again shows that this is not necessarily a linear process.

4. Find the Right Character

Your character is the heart of the story, in both a literal and figurative sense. The character is physically at the center of everything — the most important element. It's what we really care about: people, not processes.

And from the figurative standpoint, the character makes us feel something in our hearts, providing the emotional resonance that's critical to a story's success. Estela's story is not about candy manufacturing; it's about a mom looking out for the well-being of her children and customers.

So your number one job as a storyteller is to find a character your audience can relate to. The most direct way to accomplish this is to choose a character that is as close as possible to your audience in situation and circumstance. Employees will more easily relate to fellow employees, customers to other customers, insurance brokers to insurance brokers, etc.

But storytellers and audiences are naturally drawn to "bigger than life" protagonists — historical figures, sports heroes, characters from literature and film. And that's fine, as long as these characters are still relatable in some way through their values, struggles, or aspirations.

For instance, you don't have to be a Jedi Knight to relate to Luke Skywalker; you just have to understand a desire for adventure, justice, love, or a sense of identity.

5. Bring it to Resolution

Think of your story as a Hollywood blockbuster. In the end, the enemy is vanquished, the boy gets the girl, justice is served. There's a reason these movies are so popular: they give audiences what they want — a satisfactory conclusion.

Your story should not be in the style of indie or art house cinema, where the characters don't really change and problems go unresolved. The indie film may be truer to everyday life, but it's not particularly satisfying for general audiences.

So make sure your story resolves in some way. The most straightforward approach is where the character achieves the goal. Alternatively, the character may discover that the initial goal wasn't that important after all, leading to personal growth or a new direction. ("I went into this business for the money, but I soon found it was really about helping people.")

Sometimes the character is thwarted in pursuit of the goal but learns a valuable lesson. ("It was then I realized there are no shortcuts to success.")

If your story doesn't resolve in some way, look for a different story.

More to Come

This chapter covers the basics of putting together a story. It's how you might assemble a story in a laboratory setting. But we don't live and work in laboratories, so Chapter 8 will explore how you go about finding and collecting stories "in the wild."

For now, though, let's dig into what we've only touched on so far: the emotional component to storytelling, which is absolutely critical to a story's impact and success.

CHAPTER 4:
EMOTION FUELS STORIES

A few years ago I was doing a workshop for a nonprofit that fights hunger. To prepare for the day, I did some research.

I learned that one out of six people in America struggle to get enough to eat, that government programs are falling short, and that community organizations are struggling to fill the gap.

But in the workshop, I heard story after story from people on the front lines who battled the hunger problem every day. One story in particular struck me. It was from a food bank worker who said she could relate to the struggles of the people she serves because she herself started out as a *client* of that food bank. She relied on its services to help feed her own family and get back on her feet.

I was so moved that I came home and immediately made a donation to the organization. *That* is the power of emotion. Facts don't influence action the way an emotional appeal does.

Emotion Unlocks Action

We've established that emotionally charged events stick with us, in much the same way that stories do.

In fact, emotion drives decision-making. We all like to think that we are rational beings, carefully weighing all the pros and cons and making decisions based strictly on evidence and reason.

But deep down we are creatures of emotion. We're driven by feelings of fear or vanity or security. It's often said that people buy on emotion and justify with logic — facts and data are used to shore up and defend what we've already decided in our hearts.

There's even evidence to suggest that emotion doesn't just drive decision-making, it unlocks it. Neuroscientist Antonio Damasio studied a man who had sustained damage to the area of the brain that governs emotion.[12] As a result of the injury he was rendered incapable of making even the simplest decisions.[13]

The bottom line? If you want your audience to *do* something, make them *feel* something.

To Trigger Emotion, Show Emotion: A Lesson from Chrysler

So your job as a storyteller is to provoke an emotional reaction — to break down people's defenses and leave them more open to influence.

The best way to do that is to exhibit some emotion yourself, to play to people's natural sense of empathy.

In 2009, Chrysler was a company on the brink of oblivion. It went through bankruptcy, reorganization and a government bailout. Its rebirth is one of America's great comeback stories.

At a 2014 meeting with Chrysler dealers, CEO Sergio Marchionne rallied his battered troops with these words:

Those who have lived through difficulties and have seen the dark days of desperation know that the only way to get through them is by finding the values that are important in life; rediscovering a sense of belonging to a project, a community, a nation; embracing hope; looking ahead; and taking your destiny into your own hands.

If Chrysler — a company that was practically sentenced to death by the press, the financial world and the public at large — was able to do it, then there's hope for everyone. There's always a light at the end of the tunnel and there's always a way to get there. [14]

Marchionne was channeling what they were all feeling, and they were right there with him. The capstone was when he unveiled the now iconic "halftime in America" TV spot set to run on Super Bowl Sunday. As Clint Eastwood narrated:

People are out of work and they're hurting, and they're all wondering what they can do to make a comeback ... Detroit's showing us it can be done ... this country can't be knocked down with one punch. We get right back up again and when we do, the world's going to hear the roar of our engines. Yeah. It's halftime, America. And our second half is about to begin. [15]

It was undoubtedly an electric moment, but as they say in the viral video business, you won't believe what happened next ...

Can you Go Too Far with Emotion?

When the lights came back up, Marchionne concluded, "Nothing more needs to be said." And then he was so overcome, he broke down in tears and left the stage.

It could have been a disaster, but many of the dealers were themselves crying. They leapt from their seats and gave him a thunderous ovation that lasted several minutes.

Of course, this is precisely what scares so many people about public displays of emotion. The possibility of losing control, of appearing vulnerable in front of a crowd.

In most cases, it's a good idea to dial it down. A modest display of excitement, disappointment, or righteous indignation is enough to stir an audience.

But Chrysler is a special case. In the context of its near-death experience, a deeply emotional moment like this may offer the kind of cathartic group experience that's necessary to move on.

Emotion Humanizes us: A Lesson from Apple

Another important function of emotion is to humanize us, which is critical to making an authentic connection with others.

One of the biggest personalities in business was Steve Jobs. He was passionate, demanding, inspiring, temperamental, funny, and unpredictable. In other words, human.

So his successor as CEO, Tim Cook, had a decidedly tough act to follow. But over time, Cook's own persona began to emerge. At a shareholder meeting in 2014, he showcased a range of emotions — "feisty, funny and fiery," in the words of the *Los Angeles Times* headline — that helped win over his audience.[16]

He got passionate about his commitment to improving conditions for Apple's workers overseas:

> *My lifelong heroes are Martin Luther King and Bobby Kennedy. I get a lot of spears when I talk about this stuff. I don't give a crap. This is something we care deeply about. I don't think there's a company on Earth that cares more deeply about human rights than Apple does.*

Later he pushed back on a shareholder who questioned the return on investment of the company's environmental sustainability efforts:

> *When we work on making our devices accessible by the blind, I don't consider the bloody ROI. When I think about doing the right thing, I don't think about an ROI. If that's a hard line for you, then you should get out of the stock.*

Now you might debate whether these were genuine, spontaneous moments or if they were calculated for effect. Audiences, particularly skeptical reporters, can usually sniff out phoniness, and none of the coverage I saw pointed to that.

But it should go without saying that authenticity is something that cannot and should not be faked! Ultimately it's these truthful moments that endear us to people in general and leaders in particular.

How to Capitalize on Emotion in Your Storytelling

When you're formulating your stories, make sure there's an emotional component that will help you break down walls and create common ground with your audience. Here are a few ways to do that.

FOCUS ON THE "WHY"

When talking about your work or career, don't just focus on *what* you do, but *why* you do it (a concept popularized by Simon Sinek's "Start With Why").[17] Ask yourself:

- What do you love about your work?

- What makes you jump out of bed in the morning or go home satisfied at the end of the day?

- How do you make people's lives better, in ways large and small?

Center a story around those questions.

TAP INTO LOYALTY

I was interviewing a factory worker who maintains the machinery on the production line. When I asked him what he loves about his job, he looked at me like I was nuts. But as we got deeper into our conversation, I found his emotional trigger.

He talked at length about how his co-workers depend on him to keep things running smoothly. This is what mattered in his work — he didn't want to let them down. The bonds that connect employees to each other, or employees to customers and the community, often run deep and can be a rich source of emotional connection.

APPEAL TO PRIDE

Most people want to feel they're part of something bigger than themselves. A shared history or heritage, a sense of community, a commitment to quality, an affinity for a brand all carry emotional weight that can ground your stories.

CELEBRATE YOUR HEROES

Who do you admire and why? A historical figure? An athlete? A leader? Draw lessons from their struggles and achievements.

GET PERSONAL

What are your passions outside of work? Golf? Music? Gardening? Modern dance? What is it about these pursuits that brings you joy or satisfaction? And are there lessons to draw on that relate to the topic at hand? "Customer service is like executing the perfect backhand volley ..."

Share stories about your childhood or the people you're closest to. Ask yourself:

- What's the most important lesson you learned from your mother, father, daughter, or dog?

- What did you want to be when you were growing up?

- What has been your greatest disappointment or triumph?

When in doubt, you can't go wrong talking about the things and people you love.

Don't Let Modesty Stop You ...

Many of my clients are classic Midwesterners — modest and down-to-earth.

One in particular always comes up with the best stories to illustrate his points. They're drawn directly from his personal experience and they trigger an immediate emotional response.

But he's often reluctant to use these stories in his speeches to employees. "They don't want to hear this personal stuff," he says.

The thing is, they *do* want to hear that stuff. People crave a genuine connection with their leaders.

But like many executives, he's just not comfortable opening up. It's not the way he's wired.

... Or Fear

Sometimes fear is the problem. People think emotional displays are a sign of weakness. Or they worry that once they "open the floodgates" they won't be able to stop.

If fear is an issue, understand that I'm not talking about uncontrolled emotion. I'm talking about the judicious use of emotion for a strategic purpose. Which I know makes it sound contrived and manipulative, but that is not what it's about.

It's about the open expression of genuine feelings. And it doesn't have to be a "negative" emotion like anger or grief. Passion, enthusiasm, and joy go a long way too.

Also keep in mind that it's always safest to express feelings you've had a chance to process. Nobody wants to witness a breakdown. If you lost a loved one to cancer, for instance, it may be some time before you're able to discuss it in public.

So whether the issue is fear, modesty — or false modesty — don't let it hold you back. Remember, this is not about you; it's about them. From employees who need to be inspired, to customers who demand empathy, to community members who want to know you share their values, audiences expect these moments of emotional honesty.

In fact, I believe opening up and revealing your humanity is a duty of leadership.

And it's essential to delivering stories that rise above the noise of facts and data and have a real impact. Stories that truly grab people's hearts, which is the key to changing their minds.

CHAPTER 5:
STORIES AT WORK

It's one thing to understand the essential elements of storytelling; it's another to put them into action. So if you're looking for more guidance or inspiration, here are concrete examples of different kinds of stories used for different purposes and told to different audiences.

Estela and the Candy Factory

Goal: Align a team with a strategy OR promote a brand

The Estela story from Chapter 1 was an internal story designed to align employees around the goal of quality. But it could just as easily have been an external story targeted to consumers, assuring them of the company's commitment to quality.

In fact, a few years after this client engagement I saw a TV commercial from a cereal maker with the same basic plot: an employee taking pride in seeing "his" product, identified by the tracking code, on the store shelves.

It just goes to show you that a great idea doesn't have to be original!

Can you Hear me Knocking?

Goal: Establish common ground

The head of a nationwide sales force was preparing for her big speech to the troops at the company's annual meeting. One of the messages she wanted to communicate was that even in the age of digital and social media, it's still important to get out and meet with customers face to face.

Skeptics in the audience — and salespeople are notoriously skeptical — might question her credibility as a messenger. After all, she's safely ensconced in the executive suites. When was the last time she closed a sale?

So she introduced the subject by telling a story about how when she first started selling she was petrified of making cold calls — going from office to office and asking for their business. But she had a technique for managing that fear.

Whenever she got to an office building, she would immediately take the elevator to the top floor and start there. Because she knew that if she was on the ground floor it would have been far too easy to flee after the first few rejections.

By directly addressing their major objection, she disarmed her critics. She showed some humility, demonstrated that she had at least walked a few miles in their shoes, and offered a lesson on the importance of persistence in the face of adversity.

Now they were more apt to listen.

Hers wasn't the kind of story that knocks people out of their chairs, but it didn't need to be. Major movements often turn on a series of small moments.

30 Angry Men

Goal: Humanize yourself

The new CEO of a faltering truck maker was trying to drive a business turnaround. We sent him out on the road for a series of town hall meetings with employees to explain what the company needed to do to get back on track.

The first meeting was a disaster as the CEO tried to walk a roomful of disgruntled factory workers through a dry, technical PowerPoint presentation. Within a few minutes he was interrupted by a series of increasingly hostile questions that culminated in an actual shouting match.

(Well, it wasn't much of a match, since the employee was doing all the yelling, calling the CEO a liar and a fool, among other things.)

After that, we regrouped and figured out that in the next session — happening just 20 minutes later, by the way — we would have to show a little more heart.

When the next group filed in and settled down, the CEO paused for a moment, then opened up. He shared a personal story about his early days with the company as a young engineer just out of school. He discussed some of the technical hurdles he faced helping to design truck engines. He spoke of his love for the company's products, his pride in its heritage, and his hopes and dreams for its future.

Then he proceeded to deliver the presentation as planned. But the atmosphere in the room was transformed. People were still skeptical, yes, but they were at least respectful. They listened, they reasoned, and at the end of the session, several of those tough old factory workers actually shook the CEO's hand and thanked him for his visit.

This was the first halting step in thawing the relationship between management and workers, and it ultimately led to that turnaround he promised — improved financial performance, increased competitiveness, and higher levels of employee confidence and satisfaction.

And it all started with a CEO who put aside the playbook for a moment, spoke from the heart, and shared his story.

Death at the Grand Canyon

Goal: Motivate changes in behavior

Not all of my stories come from client experience. I found this one on vacation with my wife at the Grand Canyon, which is a place that's as dangerous as it is beautiful. Every year the Park Service rescues hundreds of people who get into trouble of some kind.

So they put warnings up everywhere: bring a map, stay on the trails, wear sturdy shoes, carry enough water, use sunscreen, understand the effects of altitude, and on and on and on.

But we live in an era of "warning fatigue." When was the last time you paid attention to an airline's pre-flight safety instructions or read all the cautionary language that accompanies a new piece of electronic equipment? ("Do not immerse in water!")

How do you get a message across in this environment? Through story.

One morning we headed out for a hike and noticed a small crowd gathered around a kiosk. When we got to the front of the group, we saw they were reading a flyer that tells the story of a young woman named Margaret Bradley.

Margaret was 24 years old and in excellent physical shape — she ran the Boston Marathon in just over three hours. A few weeks later she visited the Grand Canyon, went for a hike, and got into trouble.

She apparently underestimated the length of the route, didn't bring a map, and ran out of water. Sadly, Margaret ended up dying of dehydration near the canyon floor.

It's a terrible story, but it gets your attention. It has drama and emotion and a sympathetic character at its center. Margaret could be a sister, a daughter, a best friend. Any person reading this story would probably think twice about their own readiness to take on the canyon's dangers.

Now most of us don't deal every day with life-and-death matters like this. But in every organization there are consequences for our actions — *and inactions.*

Going back to the story about the IT worker in the introduction to this book, you can hammer employees all day long with policies and procedures related to safe practices online. Or you can tell a story about the guy who infected a whole department's computers, resulting in hours of downtime, lost work, and major embarrassment.

Stories provide the rationale for policy — the *why* behind the *what.* They move audiences beyond obedience to buy-in.

Another notable thing about this story is the medium: a simple flyer posted on a physical — not electronic — bulletin board. Stories don't have to be big budget affairs to be effective.

Rumble in the Jungle

Goal: Inspire a team

I'm not crazy about stories with historic or public figures as the main character. My objections are these:

1. As I've said, the most effective characters are those closest to the audience, so it's best to tell employees a story about a fellow employee, customers a story about another customer, etc.

2. It's been done to death. People tell the same stories over and over about Abe Lincoln or Mahatma Gandhi or Steve Jobs.

3. It risks being pretentious, as if you're placing your own ordinary struggles — or that of your company — on a level with, say, Nelson Mandela's. A disappointing quarter is *not* like spending 27 years in hard labor!

But what can I say? Audiences seem to enjoy them and speakers often demand them. One client asked me to work a story about Mohammed Ali into a speech he was giving. As it happens, Ali was actually a personal hero of his and he'd even met the legendary fighter, so at least there was a connection.

I found a story about Ali's famous 1974 fight against George Foreman, known as the "Rumble in the Jungle."

Ali knew he couldn't out-power Foreman, so he decided to out-smart him, most famously with the "rope-a-dope" maneuver, in which Ali hung back against the ropes, covered up, and let Foreman punch his way to exhaustion.

Ali also surprised Foreman by throwing a so-called "right-hand lead," a risky move because the punch has to travel a longer distance, giving an opponent more time to react and counter-punch.

The rope-a-dope and multiple shots to the head eventually wore Foreman down, giving Ali the victory and enabling him to reclaim the title of Heavyweight Champion of the World.

This story highlights any number of lessons: the importance of patience and discipline, brains over brawn, risk-taking, and using your opponent's strengths against him, among others.

I do, however, have my doubts about whether such stories have real staying power once the glow of inspiration wears off. They're just not as relatable as stories featuring people the audience actually knows and who are dealing with the same issues they face.

Family Treasures

Goal: Establish trust and credibility with a customer

One of the most common business stories is that of the satisfied customer, and for many companies, their Yelp or other online review pages offer a rich source of such stories.

But what about businesses that don't sell directly to consumers? I'm often asked if the storytelling rules for business-to-business enterprises are different than those for business-to-consumer companies.

There's no doubt it's a little more challenging. A brand that makes oatmeal or diapers or soup is going to have no shortage of heartwarming characters and storylines to tap. On the other hand, a company that makes machine parts for another company's machines is going to have a tougher time.

But as for the "rules," B2B storytelling is no different from B2C. You need character, conflict, resolution, and all the other elements of great storytelling.

And that includes emotion. I've seen "experts" online proclaim that price is the only consideration in a B2B transaction and that emotion doesn't even enter into the equation. Which is ridiculous. Businesses that sell to other businesses are still run and staffed by people (for the moment) and their customers are people too.

I sell my services to other businesses and I know that story and emotional connection are just as important as a track record and references. This is especially true in the realm of professional services — consulting, the law, marketing, etc. All other things being equal, people will hire the team whose personality, character, and values best mesh with their own.

And what better way to showcase that than through story?

When I worked at a PR firm, one of the teams was pitching a furniture maker for their business. So they put together a video of our people sharing stories about pieces of furniture that held sentimental value for them:

- An old rocking chair that a man inherited from his grandfather.

- A wobbly legged kitchen table that was the first stick of furniture a young couple purchased together.

- The couch where a football fan watched his team's first Super Bowl appearance.

These stories demonstrated the firm's understanding that a chair, table, or dresser is far more than the sum of its parts — the wood, glue, and upholstery from which it's made. These items are often vested with treasured memories and deep emotional attachment.

And that was enough to create a connection with the customer that not only earned trust but won the business.

Need More Help?

If you're still stumped, Part 3 of this book offers a step-by-step guide for crafting and using stories for practically any occasion, from delivering a presentation to interviewing for a job to giving a toast.

PART TWO:
ADVANCED STORYTELLING

CHAPTER 6:
HOW TO FOCUS
YOUR STORY

Character, conflict, stakes — those are all essential elements of any story. But just as important as what goes *in* to a story, is what you leave *out*. Because a perfectly good story can be absolutely ruined when it's weighed down with a lot of excess baggage.

This may be the hardest part of storytelling, because it requires us to stand outside of ourselves and look at things from the audience's perspective. To not just recount events as they happened, but to put them together in a way that's meaningful to others. To ask questions like:

- Which details will elevate the story and which will distract from it?

- Which elements should be amplified and which muted?

- What's the best way to order the events?

This is especially difficult with stories we've personally experienced. It's hard to divorce ourselves from the everyday facts of our lives and apply some objectivity. But that's the key to discovering and communicating the larger truth of our stories and giving them real impact.

Here are seven ways to focus and declutter your stories.

1. Start with a Goal

There are occasions when you might use a story simply to break the ice with an audience or humanize yourself. And that's okay.

But for the most part, stories should support and reinforce the message that you're communicating. They should have a point.

Which I know sounds obvious, but we've all sat through our share of seemingly pointless stories.

In my sketch-writing classes at Second City, they taught us that every scene starts with a strong premise. That is, it's *about* something — the underdog who tries to come out on top, the villain who takes a fall, the boy who gets the girl.

From there, every single word and action must support that premise. It has to drive the narrative forward. So you may have a joke that's guaranteed to send your audience rolling on the floor laughing, but if it doesn't address the premise, it has to be cut. "Funny for the sake of funny" is not good enough.

Similarly, every story we tell must have a goal. And every single detail must support that goal. If it doesn't, it should be cut. You may have a fascinating fact or amusing aside, but "interesting for the sake of interesting" is not good enough. Your purpose is not simply to amuse, but to change beliefs and behavior.

So make the goal your filter and question every detail of your story. Eliminate anything that's not mission-critical and keep the narrative driving ever forward.

2. Eliminate the Bit Players

Your story should focus on one main character. He or she's the star. There might be someone in a supporting role, like the employee who helps out a customer, but avoid making it an ensemble piece.

Definitely eliminate all the background players and extras. That will make it much easier for your audience to follow.

3. Avoid Tangents: How Storytelling is Like a Tree

I compare storytelling to a tree. As much as possible, you want to move in a straight line, from the base of the trunk to the top. Any time spent out on the branches (or worse, the twigs) is a tangent, a distraction, and a possible dead-end.

Take this monologue from television's Abe "Grampa" Simpson:

> *Like the time I caught the ferry to Shelbyville. I needed a new heel for m'shoe. So I decided to go to Morganville, which is what they called Shelbyville in those days. So I tied an onion to my belt, which was the style at the time. Now, to take the ferry cost a nickel, and in those days, nickels had pictures of bumblebees on 'em. "Gimme five bees for a quarter," you'd say. Now where were we ... oh yeah.*[18]

Tangents are not just an affliction of the elderly or the animated. We're all susceptible. When we're unprepared, we wander. When we're tired, we lose focus.

And when we're presenting in front of an audience, we get carried away. I've seen this over and over: a speaker gets a laugh or two and it's like a drug. They can't stop embellishing and ad-libbing and tossing in little asides. The next thing you know, a tight 20-minute talk has become a meandering 40-minute odyssey.

So if you find yourself out on a limb, take the quickest route (or root) back to your point.

4. Stick to Clear Turning Points

Life is not a Hollywood movie. Situations don't always turn on a dime in an instant cause-and-effect relationship: "When the project failed, Sam got a brilliant idea for a whole new approach."

In real life, there are many twists and turns along the way. Maybe Sam shopped his idea around, and then it went through a couple of committees and some pilot testing, was shelved for a while, and then later refined.

We don't need all those details. (Unless your story is about the trial-and-error process or corporate bureaucracy.)

If you asked me how the S&P 500 did last year, would you want to hear a blow-by-blow account of each day's ups and downs? Of course not. You'd expect a summary of the major trends.

In the same way, your story does not need to document every turning point. Pick one, and make that your focus.

5. Details, Details: Separating the Good from the Bad

Stephen King says that "belief and reader absorption comes in the details."[19] And that's especially true if you're a bestselling author working on your next 600-page thriller.

For most of us, too many details — or too many of the wrong kind of details — can weigh a story down. So how do you distinguish between the details that bring a story to life and those that just clutter it up?

Here's some guidance.

USE (BRIEF) DETAILS TO SET THE SCENE

It's important to give your audience a sense of time and place. "It was Southern California in the late 70s" says a lot. Telling us the day of the week, the weather and the exact street corner is less helpful.

Remember, it's a story, not an affidavit.

OFFER SENSORY DETAILS TO BRING A STORY TO LIFE

Details that stimulate our sense memory can be an effective way to bring people into your story:

- When I asked him for a raise, he sat stone-faced, and for an endless moment the only sound in the room was the tick-tick-tick of the clock on the wall.

- The familiar smell drifted from the breakroom microwave all the way down the hall to Frank's cubicle. Beth's making popcorn. Again.

- The presentation was not going well. I felt a cold bead of sweat trickle down the small of my back.

Think about a particular sight, sound, smell, taste, or feel that might click, as it were, with the listener or reader.

SIMPLIFY DATES

Dates tend to trip people up. Was it a Tuesday or a Wednesday? The 12th or the 14th? July or August? It rarely matters. Instead of saying "the deal that was signed on March 22, 2005," you can just call it "the 2005 deal."

And the farther back in time you go, the less precise you need to be. Saying a company was founded in 1920 is sufficient to communicate that it's been around a long time. You might even say it was founded "a century ago." Yes, approximations are okay in storytelling!

The only time a precise date matters is when it's relevant to the point of your story. "I started my new job on Wall Street … on September 11, 2001."

MAKE NUMBERS MORE MEANINGFUL

Raw numbers should be rounded: "several hundred" works better than "278." Percentages should be converted: "half" beats "53%." And big numbers should be scaled: "one out of five Americans" is easier to grasp than "63 million people."

OMIT PROPER NOUNS

Just about anything in capital letters is ripe for trimming, starting with names. Minor characters in your story don't need to be named, especially if they make a one-time appearance. You can just call them "the bank manager" or "the CEO."

(And while we're at it, we don't need to know their precise relationship to you or your main character. When it's your third cousin on your mother's side, calling him your "cousin" or "a relative" will do just fine.)

The same goes for job titles, department names, and company names. A good rule of thumb is "name the known and omit the obscure." So if you're talking about a company nobody's ever heard of, just refer to it by what it does: "a small venture capital firm." If it's Google or Kraft, go ahead and name them.

If your character has a big long job title like Assistant Vice President of Sales, Midwest Region, just say he's in sales. Long department names? Shorthand them. HR won't like that, but you're not creating an org chart.

6. Cut the Exposition

To grab your audience from the start, eliminate elaborate setups and jump right into the action: "I stood there, petrified, as the CEO chewed me out in front of the whole group."

Once you've got their attention, you can jump back in time to get them up to speed.

Think of it as the difference between a movie like *Gone With the Wind*, where we have a long series of title cards introducing us to the story, versus any James Bond film, which starts with a chase or a punch in the face.

And whatever you do, don't begin with, "This is a story about ..." Just start telling the story.

7. It's Okay to Lie (Sort Of)

We've all heard the saying, "Don't let the truth get in the way of a good story." That doesn't mean you should lie, of course. It just means simplifying things for the sake of the audience experience.

Storyteller Matthew Dicks talks about the essential "lies" necessary for effective storytelling.[20] Omitting irrelevant details, compressing the timeline, even changing the order of events, are all fair game. I was talking to an audience in Denver and mentioned that I hadn't been skiing in 10 years and showed a picture of me up on the mountain in full gear.

But it was a LIE! I actually hadn't been skiing in 9 years, not 10. And get this: the photo wasn't even from that trip 9 years before — it was actually from another trip 14 years before!

Would fully disclosing those details make the story more honest? Technically, maybe. Would it have disrupted the narrative flow? Absolutely.

There's a big difference between simplifying a story and altering its fundamental truth. Where do you draw the line? A good test is to ask yourself whether someone who was there to witness the events would recognize your version as fair and truthful.

Be Ruthless in Refining Your Stories

The funniest comment I ever got from an audience member was a tweet that said, "Everybody's grandma should hear Rob Biesenbach talk about storytelling!"

Now I've got nothing against grandmas. And for the record, I've seen millennials drag out stories beyond reason. But this is an aspect of storytelling that I'm fanatical about. Probably because I'm an impatient person.

I don't think I'm alone in that — especially in this era of easy distraction. So I would much rather err toward skimping on the details than risk boring my audience.

Each of us has to draw our own line in the sand.

CHAPTER 7:
HOW TO PRESERVE THE INTEGRITY OF YOUR STORIES

Storytelling, like art, is about having the courage to make bold choices, and the conviction to stand by those choices.

That's not easy. Especially in a world that discourages risk-taking and rewards fitting in.

So here I want to share two important storytelling experiences I've had and the lessons they can teach us about making and keeping our stories as pure and powerful as possible.

Not Your Grandfather's Anniversary Celebration

A few years ago I had the opportunity to work on a dream project for a law firm that wanted to commemorate its 25th year in business.

Anniversaries are the kind of thing that few people outside a company's founders find interesting. And the tactics used to mark these occasions are equally uninspired — self-congratulatory press releases, newsletter articles, and logoed knick-knacks.

But this firm, Freeborn & Peters, was willing to do something different. A creative partner and I worked with them to produce a big, beautiful book full of stories from the firm's history. Which doesn't sound all that innovative, but we made "the usual" unusual.

Instead of an inward-facing look at the firm's many wonderful accomplishments, we turned the spotlight outward, to shine on their clients. And we didn't just do boring, straightforward profiles of those organizations, we brought them to life by putting character and story front and center.

PUT THE STORY FIRST ...

Our goal was to tell stories with mass appeal, like the kind you might read in a popular magazine. For instance, one of their attorneys helped resolve a decades-old dispute over the use of a rail yard in Chicago. Here's how our story opened:

> *First it belonged to the sea. Then it belonged to the railroads. Now it belongs to the people. What a long, strange trip it has been for the 25-acre parcel of land that is home to Chicago's renowned Millennium Park, an award-winning center for art, music and architecture ... Quite a distinction for a site that spent most of its existence under water.*

As the story unfolded, it touched on Abraham Lincoln, the Great Chicago Fire, Daniel Burnham, and more — all leading up to the deal that made the park possible.

Other stories in the book profiled the rise of a sandwich empire from Jimmy John Liautaud's garage, described how a power company helped save Christmas on Fiji and, believe it or not, traced the history of waste disposal from ancient Athens to the modern age.

As we developed the book over the course of a year, the firm's attorneys came to us with lots of ideas. But our cardinal rule — story first — meant many of those concepts didn't make the cut.

... AND SELF-INTEREST LAST

In each story, when we got around to talking about the firm's role in helping the client succeed, it was usually confined to a sentence or two near the end, often in an "Oh, by the way" fashion.

There was no deep dive into intricate matters of the law, no legal jargon, no Latin, no case citations. We didn't even name the attorneys involved, which raised a few eyebrows.

Why? Because it wasn't about the firm. It wasn't about hitting people over the head with a sales pitch. It was about engaging readers.

Our message was in the subtext. As the old saying goes, "Judge us by the company we keep." Or, more precisely, "Just look at the cool clients who trust us with their business! Wouldn't you like to be our client too?"

And it worked. People actually read the thing! We got a ton of positive feedback, we won several awards, and the firm even picked up some big new pieces of business as a direct result of the book.

RESTRICT THE APPROVAL PROCESS

A major key to our success was that we limited the number of people who were involved. The "editorial board" for the project consisted of just two of the firm's partners, who worked with us to brainstorm ideas, review drafts, and approve the final content.

Other attorneys would have an opportunity to weigh in on stories that pertained to their clients, but our small committee exercised final judgment. If a suggested revision undermined the integrity of the story, it was rejected.

The result was a product mostly untainted by the kinds of compromises that spoil good storytelling.

A Story That Rises Above the Rest

One of the best corporate stories I've seen is a video for the global consulting firm Deloitte, for whom I did a storytelling workshop.

Designed to promote the firm's crisis management practice, the video focuses on a not-so-ordinary day in the life of a business person:

> *A man wakes to his alarm clock and thinks through his priorities for the day — meetings, phone calls, the usual. Over breakfast with his family, all the phones start ringing at once. He turns on the TV to find that he and his company are the subjects of an overseas bribery investigation. He soon realizes that today is not just another day — his wife ushers their concerned children from the room, he's mobbed on the street by reporters, the company's stock plunges. His world spins out of control.*[21]

It's a powerful video, from the scriptwriting to the cinematography. But the best thing about it? It tells *one* story about *one* character facing *one* specific challenge.

NARROWER IS BETTER

The fact that this story made it through the vast approval chain of this giant company is a miracle. I wasn't there to witness the process, but based on my experience over many years, I can imagine how it went.

Someone, somewhere along the line must have expressed concern that the video was too narrowly focused. After all, financial crimes are just one of many crises Deloitte's experts can handle. Shouldn't the video be more comprehensive?

If that person had his way, the video would read like a fact sheet, describing all the different kinds of crisis work Deloitte does, along with the number of countries in which it operates, the full range of services it offers, and a bunch of other information.

But none of that will grab an audience the way a story does. The video's creators clearly understood that and stuck to their guns. Bravo to them.

MAKE THE SPECIFIC UNIVERSAL

Common sense might suggest that the more general you are in your storytelling, the more likely you'll appeal to a wider audience. But actually, great filmmakers know the opposite to be true.

Think about the stories you love best. Do you have to understand the science of space travel to enjoy *Star Trek*? Do you need to know the ins and outs of the real estate business to appreciate *Glengarry Glen Ross*? Or the intricacies of the military justice system to comprehend *A Few Good Men*?

Of course not. Because all those details are simply the backdrop to timeless stories featuring relatable characters dealing with universal struggles — like the quest for adventure, the desire for recognition, or the search for truth.

The Deloitte video works for the same reason. Few of us have been accused of financial fraud or been hounded by reporters shoving microphones in our direction. But most of us have faced a crisis of some kind, felt frustrated over events out of our control, and dealt with the effects of stress on ourselves and those around us.

The specifics help ground the stories in reality, but those details are transcended by the universal truths conveyed.

TRUST YOUR AUDIENCE

In the end, it comes down to trust.

In the improv world, there's a concept known as "playing to the top of your intelligence." What that means is, you don't go for the dumb joke or the obvious choice. You play smart and trust that your audience will understand.

In Deloitte's case, they trust that viewers will recognize that the video is not a comprehensive representation of the breadth and depth of the firm's crisis services. They trust that the story will be enough to intrigue prospects and make them want to know more. They trust that any client — or client worth having — will get it.

Your Mission: Defend the Integrity of Your Story

Of course, a story doesn't achieve its full potential until it's shared — whether in a presentation, online, in your marketing materials, or elsewhere. And if you happen to work in an organization of any size, before you can share it you'll probably need to run that story by other people to get it approved.

And that is where great stories go to die — the meat grinder that is the corporate approval process.

Among the hurdles you may face:

- HR managers who push for inclusiveness. ("You can't feature this department without naming all five!").

- Lawyers who load up stories with unnecessary and distracting detail.

- Committees that water them down in a misguided effort to make them more universal.

These are the people who can suck the life out of a great story.

Your job is to defend your story from these outside forces and preserve its basic integrity. How do you do that? Through negotiation. Here are some tips:

- **Prioritize what's important.** Take a stand on the big issues like character, conflict, stakes, and emotion.

- **Let go of the little things.** Be willing to compromise on the smaller things that may slow down your story but not stop it in its tracks — the odd department name or other non-essential information people insist upon.

- **Have a conversation.** Seek explanation for the changes people want to make. Be open to the idea that their reasoning may actually have some validity.

- **Cite evidence.** Support your choices by pointing to some of the evidence cited in this book on the power of story and emotion and their effect on the brain.

- **Keep it positive.** Steer the conversation into positive territory. Instead of it being about what you *can't* do, make it about what you *can* do.

In the end, you will probably have to let go of the desire for perfection. But do your best to keep it as close to perfect as reasonably possible.

CHAPTER 8:
HOW AND WHERE TO FIND GREAT STORIES

The worst time to look for a story is when you really need one.

You're up against a deadline — maybe you've got a big presentation due or job interview to prep for — and you find yourself saying, "If only I had a great story to illustrate this point …"

So you do an online search, entering a term like "stories about teamwork," and you end up with one of the following outcomes:

- You find a story that everyone's heard before. Eye rolls ensue.

- The story doesn't quite fit and feels shoehorned in. (Because it is.)

- You deliver the story lifelessly, without enthusiasm. Because you're not connected to it.

Don't let this happen to you!

To be an effective communicator, you have to be a lifelong collector of stories, so when you really need one, it's right there for you, ready to be shared.

The key to building your collection is having a clear understanding of who you are and what you're about — if you're the "quality" guy, you'll look for stories on that topic. That will help you focus your efforts.

From there it's a matter of keeping your antennae up, knowing where and how to dig for stories, and having some kind of system to store and retrieve them.

But first let's talk a little more about the problem with Googling for stories.

What's So Wrong with Finding Stories Online?

Attend enough conferences and you'll hear the same stories over and over again. A few of the most overused ones begin like this:

- *A professor fills a jar with rocks and asks his students if they think it's full ...*

- *A battleship spots a light from an approaching vessel and orders it to adjust course ...*

- *A young man comes upon thousands of starfish washed up on the beach and throws one back into the water. An older man scoffs, telling him he can't possibly save them all ...*

If you're one of the few who hasn't heard these timeworn tales, here are the payoffs (*spoiler alert*):

- *The jar isn't full until it's filled with gravel, sand and water.*[22]

- *The other "ship" is actually a lighthouse.*[23]

- *The young man educates the older one on how saving just one life makes a difference.*[24]

That last one is told so many times it's become a bit of an "in-joke" among professional speakers. And it's morphed into countless variations where the starfish thrower is an old man, a little girl — even Jesus!

If you must search online for your story, at least try to find one that doesn't turn up hundreds of thousands of Google hits like these three do.

By the way, another danger of hasty, last-minute Internet research is that you end up spreading false information. For years, "experts" have regaled audiences with the story of the Chevy Nova which, according to (urban) legend, flopped in Latin America because the name means "no go" in Spanish.

As even a casual Google search will show, the story is itself a non-starter.[25] While "nova" may literally mean "no go," no native Spanish speaker would interpret it that way.

So please, if you must Google, do so responsibly. But it's better to follow these six steps.

1. Use Your Goals and Priorities as a Filter

When you become attuned to stories, you'll find that everyday life offers a veritable firehose of material coming your way. You'll discover relatable stories on your favorite TV shows, while waiting in line at Starbucks, and in conversation with friends and co-workers.

In fact, you'll quickly become inundated with stories ... unless you have a filter.

What's your filter? It's the handful of things that constitute your focus — for yourself or for your business. It goes by many names: goals, strategies, priorities, value proposition, brand, selling points, key messages, core strengths, etc. For example:

- A business that has built its reputation on fast and reliable service.

- A job candidate whose strengths are creativity, resourcefulness, and follow-through.

- A department head who's trying to drive innovation and collaboration.

These people should be on the lookout for stories that illustrate those points. For me, my mission is to help people become more skilled, confident communicators, so I'm always watchful for stories about persuasion techniques, listening, body language, and other communication-related matters.

2. Keep Your Antennae Up

Once you've established your filter, be alert for situations in your everyday life that might make a good story — at the gym or the grocery story, in the car or on the bus, whenever you're out and about. I've found stories in all kinds of places:

- In Pilates class I learned a great lesson about how people don't listen. They come to class so frequently they've practically memorized the routine. So when the instructor changes things up, they don't adapt. That's because they're not truly listening — they are literally "going through the motions."

- On vacation I found the Grand Canyon story from Chapter 5, which offers a lesson on how to rise above the noise and motivate changes in behavior.

- At parties I've learned countless lessons on the art of conversation that I've turned into stories about how to authentically connect with others. And how not to! (Don't worry, I never name names.)

3. Read and Explore

If you read mainly business books and trade journals, try casting a wider net. Look outside your industry or profession. Pick up a magazine you've never read or check out a blog on a subject you've never explored. Inspiration can come from the most surprising places.

Read non-business books, like biographies and memoirs — those are filled with stories few people have heard. Or try a novel.

Beyond reading, see a play, go to the symphony, attend a dance recital, take a pottery class, learn the guitar, study martial arts — the options are endless.

The point is to try something different from what you normally do and see where the process of discovery takes you.

4. Interview Others

Your employees, customers, members, volunteers, and other constituents are a rich source of stories. Sometimes those stories come to you — in the form of letters, emails, and online reviews. Other times you may have to hunt for them.

Put together a list of possible "characters" from your chosen audience. Think about people who have a positive point of view and who are good at expressing themselves. Then sit down and interview them. Record it on video if you can for sharing with others.

Your customers will appreciate a peek into the lives of the people behind the product. Your employees will benefit from stories from satisfied (and unsatisfied) customers. Donors will be inspired by the stories of those they've helped.

Sometimes the process will be simple and straightforward. If you already basically know the story, it's a matter of getting your interview subjects to put it into their own words and give it some texture and personality.

Other times your hunt becomes more of a fishing expedition. You don't know what you're looking for, you just know you've got a great character who probably has something important to say.

In that case, here are a few of my favorite interview questions (which are similar to those I recommend in Chapter 4 for tapping into emotion):

- What did you want to be when you were growing up?

- What does your child think you do?

- What's the best lesson you learned from a parent, friend, or mentor?

- How did you get started?

- What do you love about your job?

- How does what you do make a difference to others?

- What frustrates you?

- What makes you proud?

- Who are your heroes and why?

Sometimes it takes a lot of digging. You may have to interview a bunch of characters before you strike gold, but the result is worth it.

5. Draw on Your Personal Experience

Some of the best stories are the ones drawn from our own personal experience. Telling a personal story means you'll be more connected to the material, which makes your delivery more authentic and helps the audience better connect to you. (It also practically guarantees your story will be original!)

But isn't it wrong to talk about yourself? Well, if the story is *only* about you, if you position yourself as an infallible hero, if it's not relevant to your audience's concerns ... then yes, you should not tell a story about yourself. That would be self-indulgent. (In Chapter 14 I discuss how to avoid sounding like a jerk when telling your story.)

Let's assume you're a reasonably humble and self-aware person. Start by asking yourself the questions in the previous section. Or enlist someone to interview you. Try thinking through some of the major milestones of your life — school, work, relationships — and see what's there.

Or try writing. Some of my best stories emerge as I'm blogging, writing books, or putting together speeches. Even if you have no interest in publishing your thoughts for the world to see, you can always create a private blog or even a handwritten journal.

Write about anything — a treasured childhood toy or memory, your first house, your best vacation, your favorite teacher, an influential person in your life, a dream you have for the future. Not only will this exercise turn up some interesting stories, it may actually be therapeutic!

6. Find a System for Storing Your Stories

As you collect your stories, you need some way to retrieve them when you need them. So make sure you're organizing them somewhere. There are a lot of free apps you can use to take, store, and organize notes. You can even tag them by topic or audience or whatever's most helpful.

Or maybe you're a spreadsheet person — that works too.

One thing I wouldn't rely on too heavily is your brain. Few things are worse than having a brilliant idea and forgetting what it was.

The point is to never be caught with your back against the wall, having to resort to Google or dusting off some tired old anecdote about Thomas Edison that we've all heard before.

CHAPTER 9:
STORY'S COUSINS: COMPARISON, ANALOGY, AND METAPHOR

The point of storytelling is to bring more meaning to our words and greater impact to our ideas. But a full-fledged story isn't the only way to accomplish that.

Often a simple turn of phrase, an apt analogy, or the right metaphor is enough to "move the needle" (see what I did there?) on audience understanding, retention, and buy-in. And even though they land short of story, figures of speech and evocative language fire our imagination in much the same way that stories do.

Let's take a look at some of these "kissing cousins" to story.

Choose Words that Stimulate the Senses

One of my most-used words is "cool." It's a term that has stood the test of time compared to some of its synonyms, such as the briefly fashionable "groovy." And it's fairly universal — unlike, say, "wicked," which is mainly a New England thing.

It turns out there's a reason. Wharton professor and author Jonah Goldberg co-published a study finding that words like "cool" evoke a sensory response and "our senses (e.g., sight, smell, and touch) have a big impact on linguistic success."[26]

So for that reason, a "sharp" increase beats a "sudden" one, a "bright" future seems, well, *"sunnier"* than a "promising" one, and a "sour" disposition is more memorable than a "negative" one.

And don't forget the visual sense. Social media expert and master communicator Paul Gillin advocates the use of more visually evocative verbs. So the words *climb* or *soar* are better than *rise*; *grab* or *seize* are superior to *take*; and *hurl* and *toss* beat *throw*.[27]

These words also have the advantage of being more precise.

One source of inspiration for sharpening your language is literature. When I read books, I'm constantly highlighting imaginative turns of phrase. Here are a few excerpts from a recent read, Anthony Doerr's *All the Light We Cannot See*, describing the World War II bombardment of a French town:

> *Flames **scamper** up the walls ... fires **pool** and **strut** [and] **splash** into alleys ... earth and granite **spout** into the sky.*[28]

So as you craft your stories, pay special attention to the words you choose. A little clever wordplay can go a long way.

Use Metaphor and Analogy to Clarify

In communicating the power of metaphor, it's hard to top this headline: "Why Metaphors Beat the Snot Out of

Facts When it Comes to Motivating Action." The author, Douglas Van Praet, is a brand strategist and expert on the subconscious mind. He breaks it down this way:

> *Provocative metaphors, much like artful stories, are among the most impactful tools of influence ever, because they evoke feelings that bypass critical thinking. And they easily transform abstract ideas into tangible, simpler more relatable representations.*[29]

It's why love is a "battlefield," a shaky argument is a "house of cards" and a sensitive person is a "delicate flower." Metaphors serve as a universal shorthand for communicating ideas.

Analogies play a similar role. In 1962, John F. Kennedy delivered a famous speech in which he vowed that America would send a man to the Moon by the end of the decade.[30] The text is filled with figures of speech designed to bring abstract concepts "to Earth."

In one example, he said a new booster rocket possessed "power equivalent to 10,000 automobiles with their accelerators on the floor." He also made ample use of metaphor, describing the space mission as "set[ting] sail on this new sea," and comparison, which we'll tackle next.

Make Comparisons to Simplify Large Numbers

Big numbers can be hard for most people to grasp, so it's important to offer some scale by comparing them to everyday touchpoints. To capture the size of a new rocket assembly building, Kennedy said it was "as tall as a 48-story structure, as wide as a city block, and as long as two lengths of this field."

That covers height, width, and length — what about area? Acreage is a measure that never quite computes for me. Wildfires are always described as destroying thousands of acres of forest. But how many people really know what an acre is — let alone 20,000?

Farmers and ranchers, perhaps. Most other people could probably use a familiar reference point, like "the size of Manhattan." Even square miles would be easier to visualize.

Volume can be a tricky one. When I was on a road trip through the upper Great Lakes area, I came upon an interpretive plaque that explained how much water Lake Superior holds. The total volume is 3 quadrillion gallons. That's a lot of water, right? But how much is it really?

For some reason, liquid volume is always compared to a given number of Olympic-sized swimming pools. Would knowing that 3 quadrillion gallons equates to 4.5 billion Olympic-sized swimming pools put things in perspective? Probably not.

But what if I told you (per the helpful sign) that Lake Superior contains enough water to cover all of North and South America a foot deep? Now that's an amount you can really put your arms around (figuratively, at least).

It's all about giving abstract numbers a human scale. It's why charitable organizations say you can feed or educate a child for the price of your morning cup of coffee.

Let Your Words Fuel Your Stories

All of these devices alone are powerful ways to get your point across. But they can also help propel your stories and boost audience understanding.

It's not, as they say, rocket science.

CHAPTER 10:
THE DARK SIDE OF STORYTELLING

If a blimp crashes in Florida, does it make a sound? Are stories just lies? Does the truth matter?

Even as I advocate for more and better storytelling in business, I can't help but feel some discomfort over how stories are so often misused and abused. I suppose like any other tool, stories can be used for purposes both good and evil.

Let's explore a few of the hazards surrounding storytelling and how to navigate around them.

Do Stories Make Facts Irrelevant?

We've all been in pointless arguments where it seems no amount of evidence will convince the other side. For every fact we cite, they stubbornly dig in to their beliefs. In response to hard statistics, they offer vague anecdotes ("This happened to a friend of a friend"). Any appeal to cool reason is met with white-hot emotion.

This is basic human nature. According to neuroscientist Sam Wang, "[O]ur brains fit facts into established mental frameworks. We tend to remember news that accords with our worldview, and discount statements that contradict it."[31]

In other words, our brains lie to us.

Does this mean facts don't matter? I'd hate to live in a world where that was the case!

Yes, there are those who seek to manipulate others through appeals to fear or vanity or security. For the rest of us — I'd like to believe *most* of us — there's a moral imperative at work.

And a practical one. Even in an age of "alternative facts," I believe a story not based on truth will only get you so far in the long run.

A Rule for Storytellers: Do No Harm

Storytelling is full of gray areas, and it's no wonder. We use the label "story" both for fact-checked articles appearing in an established newspaper and for tall tales told around the campfire.

As stories take hold in the popular imagination, separating fact from fiction can be difficult.

One of the many iconic skyscrapers in Chicago is the old Montgomery Ward headquarters building. Its most distinctive feature is that while the exterior is mostly glass, all four corners — typically the premium space in any building — are covered in stone, obliterating the sweeping views tenants crave.

If you believe the city tour guides, that's because the founder was an egalitarian who felt that prestigious corner offices needlessly set executives apart from other workers. It's a great story — a "concrete" demonstration of one company's collegial culture.

Sadly, it doesn't appear to be true. The real reason for the unusual design was structural — the masonry helped brace the building, making interior columns unnecessary and freeing up usable office space inside.

Does the truth matter here? It depends. If the company itself touted the legend (and I've found no evidence that it did), that could raise a question of credibility.

If, on the other hand, they didn't aggressively go out and correct the public record every time someone passed along the tale, I think that might fall under the "do no harm" clause for storytelling (which I just made up). It's not like falsifying a balance sheet, after all.

Meanwhile, it's a good idea to view with some skepticism any story that begins, "Legend has it," which is a fancy way of saying, "We have no evidence for this, but it sure sounds great!"

The Tyranny of the Narrative

Now about that blimp. During the 2012 presidential campaign, a blimp displaying an ad for Mitt Romney crashed in Florida.[32] Luckily, no one was hurt. But it's exactly the kind of incident that might get huge play in the media, as it makes an irresistible metaphor for a flailing campaign.

And for many months the campaign *was* flailing. They just couldn't catch a break, and the negative media coverage reflected that. There was even a hashtag for it: #RomneyShambles.

But at this particular moment, the campaign was on a bit of a roll — enjoying what some called "Mittmentum" (seriously). They were riding the wave of one of the most compelling narratives there is: the comeback story.

Whether they were actually experiencing a real comeback is debatable — the polling data suggested otherwise. But no matter! The narrative prevailed and the blimp barely registered a blip.

And this is what happens with political coverage. Reporters can only write the same story for so long. Today you're a winner, tomorrow you're a loser. Eventually the narrative's pendulum swings back. As Dartmouth Professor Brendan Nyhan puts it:

> *[P]rofessional and commercial incentives do exist for journalists to emphasize the drama of a race. By whatever conscious or unconscious means, these may increase journalists' susceptibility to a 'momentum' narrative despite its tenuous basis in fact.*[33]

So when you're down, every stumble gets blown out of proportion and every good thing you do is ignored (or seen as a cynical attempt to change the narrative). And when you're up, all your warts are overlooked (or called beauty marks).

The lessons? For consumers of stories, beware the herd mentality. When the story sounds too good — or bad — to be true, check the underlying facts.

And when the story's about you or your company? When you're riding high, enjoy it. But don't get too comfortable — what the narrative giveth, the narrative taketh away.

That said, when you can't seem to catch a break, keep your head down and work your way through it. Because as sure as sharks will swarm next summer off the coast of Florida, your moment in the uncomfortable spotlight will eventually pass.

Blurred Lines: The Brian Williams Effect

Moving from blimps to helicopters, newscaster Brian Williams came under significant metaphorical fire in 2015 when he said he came under actual fire in a war zone.[34] The ensuing scandal eventually led to his departure as anchor of NBC's Nightly News.

The facts of the actual incident are murky and much disputed. The one thing we know is that Williams was covering the Iraq War in 2003 and a helicopter was hit by enemy fire.

Whether that was a helicopter flying just ahead of his or a half-hour ahead or was the one he himself was aboard depends on whose story you believe. Accounts vary, including his own. It seems the more he told the story, the closer he got to the action and the farther he got from the truth.

Did Williams lie outright or simply misremember? Further scrutiny of his reporting found other "inconsistencies" on record, but for our purposes I don't care which it was, because it points to an important lesson for storytellers.

As Sam Wang reminds us, memories don't just fade, they are continuously processed, reprocessed, and overwritten in our heads.[35] Every time we tell a story, it gets reshaped and scrambled.

Neurobiologist James McGaugh puts it this way:

All memory ... is colored with bits of life experiences. When people recall, they are reconstructing ... It doesn't mean it's totally false. It means that they're telling a story about themselves and they're integrating things they really do remember in detail, with things that are generally true.[36]

Whether this applies in Williams' case I don't know. But I do know from personal experience that stories tend to "drift" over time as they're retold. I've told some stories dozens of times and will often go back to the original, contemporaneous account (in a book or blog post) to discover that some details have morphed.

Usually they are small, inconsequential matters — a date or a number. The essential truth of the story is unchanged. But it reminds me to be careful, and to make sure I don't start unconsciously fudging the important things.

The lesson for storytellers is to fact-check your stories. Run your account by others who were there. Write them down someplace so you'll have a record.

And be especially mindful of how you portray your role in the events. It's natural to want to make yourself more and more the center of a story, but that can be dangerous territory, as Brian Williams found.

Blurred Lines II: Experience vs. Memory

Let's end on another cautionary note.

My father was a soldier with the US Army's heralded 101st Airborne Division. As part of his training, he jumped out of a lot of airplanes.

When I was three years old, we were living off-base in a high-rise apartment. One morning I toddled out to the balcony and proceeded to get my head stuck between the railings.

So my father went up to the roof of the building, parachuted down, and on his way to the ground managed to shove my head back through the rails.

As you may have guessed, at least some of this story is false.

I did indeed get my head stuck in that railing, but the process of getting unstuck was far less dramatic. And yet I remember my Dad in the parachute as vividly as I recall the panicked feeling that I'd be stuck there forever.

Why? Because our brains are storytelling machines and it fit the narrative of my worldview as a child. Dad was my hero, he jumped out of planes for the Army (the heavy, bronze paratrooper "trophies" that stood on our bookshelf were an endless source of fascination for me), so naturally he would come to my rescue in that way.

But here's the thing: even for the "true" part of the story I can't say for sure whether I actually remember experiencing it or if that memory was "planted" in my brain by my family's constant retelling of it over the dinner table.

And you may be thinking, "Sure, it's easy to put one over on a toddler." But researchers have found that it's relatively easy to plant false memories in people's minds.[37]

Add time to the equation and you can see how the line between story and experience gets blurred.

Proceed With Caution

For storytellers, the lesson again is to be careful about exaggerating — and even inventing — your role in the events you're describing. For me, I typically err toward minimizing my role, talking in terms of "we" or "the team."

It doesn't diminish the story in any way, and it probably adds a dose of humility to a tale that otherwise might be considered "too good to be true."

PART THREE:
APPLIED STORYTELLING

CHAPTER 11:
HOW TO TELL YOUR
COMPANY'S ORIGIN STORY

Every business needs its "origin" story. One that explains how and why it was founded, traces its history, communicates its purpose, and offers a glimpse of the people (characters) behind the brand.

It helps humanize the business in the eyes of potential customers, employees, and other key audiences — which is important because most humans prefer to deal with other humans, not institutions.

(Of course, the same goes for any organization, including nonprofits, associations — perhaps even government entities — but for simplicity's sake I'll be using the words company or business here.)

If you're a business owner or operate a business, here is some guidance on creating or improving your company's story.

All the Normal Storytelling Rules Apply

The origin story requires all the basic elements outlined in this book: character, goal, challenge, resolution, conflict, stakes, and emotional investment.

And it brings with it all the usual challenges, from figuring out which details to focus on (especially hard for companies that have a long history to sort through), to maintaining some level of objectivity, to avoiding blatant self-promotion.

The solution lies in thinking first about what the audience wants — they're less interested in *you* than in what you can do for *them*. Then you want to establish a theme for the story that's tied to the organization's goals or brand promise.

So whatever you want to be known for, whether it's innovation or quality or service or value, that must be threaded through the narrative. It can also serve as the filter for eliminating clutter.

The Opposite of Story: The Corporate Timeline

Companies often populate their websites and headquarters hallways with lengthy timelines stuffed with events of varying degrees of significance — ground-breakings, acquisitions, expansions, reorganizations, sales milestones, awards, and the like.

I have a natural aversion to timelines, which can probably be traced to a middle school history teacher who made us construct elaborate timelines of colonial history. As an adult I marvel at how little of that history I retained. I'd be hard pressed to explain the significance of the Stamp Act or the Whiskey Rebellion, let alone tell you the day, month and year in which they happened!

And that's because data points do not stick. Stories and characters do.

If you must create a timeline, be a little discriminating about the events you feature. The day your founder was hiking through a remote canyon, discovered an untapped vein of precious metal deposits, and went into town to stake his claim? That's a keeper!

The time you consolidated your procurement and supply chain management functions? Not so much.

And do your best to give the events some flavor — conflict, drama, human interest.

The bottom line is, customers and the public don't care about these milestones nearly as much as the company does. (And honestly, few in the company care much either.)

This is where stories come in. Think about the purpose of your timeline. Is it to demonstrate that the organization has been around a long time and is thus a reliable partner that customers and investors can count on? Is it designed to show a track record of innovation? Or trace the company's steady growth from a lemonade stand to a multinational enterprise?

All of those goals can be captured much more effectively (and entertainingly) in a story.

Examples of Company Origin Stories

Company stories usually show up in the "About Us" section of corporate websites, which are typically the most visited pages on any site, so it's important to get them right.

These stories typically unfold in a predictable pattern:

- The founder or founders are introduced.

- They make a discovery or solve a problem that vexes most people, or they vow to do business in a different way.

- They turn their idea into a product, service, or business.

- The business grows, expands, and transforms into a community leader, industry powerhouse, global enterprise, etc.

- Not surprisingly, for all its success, the company still operates according to the values it was founded upon.

It's a classic approach, but just because it's predictable doesn't make it wrong. Part of the power of stories is that they scratch a subconscious itch in the listener's mind — an expectation that a story will proceed and "pay off" in a certain fashion.

JOHN DEERE

Here's a prime example from John Deere:

The Plow That Started it All

In 1837 our founder, John Deere, was a typical blacksmith turning out hayforks, horseshoes, and other essentials for life on the prairie.

Then one day, a broken steel sawmill blade gave him an opportunity. He knew that days in the field were difficult for farmers near his home in Grand Detour, Illinois, because they had to interrupt their work to clean the sticky prairie soil off of their cast-iron plows. He also knew that the soil would slide easily off of a highly polished steel moldboard. Steel was scarce in the area, so Deere fashioned a moldboard out of the second-hand blade.

Now, 175 years later, the company that grew out of the success of this innovative plow continues to manufacture advanced equipment to help those who work with the land accomplish their tasks better and faster.[38]

It's a good story. You've got a character starting from humble roots, a challenge (farmers must interrupt their work to clean their plow blades), and a solution. You also have a theme — innovation — that's threaded throughout the rest of the story.

SUBWAY

Sandwich chain Subway follows the same basic formula:

The Seventeen-Year-Old Entrepreneur

Back in 1965, Fred DeLuca set out to fulfill his dream of becoming a medical doctor. Searching for a way to help pay for his education, a family friend suggested he open a submarine sandwich shop.

With a loan of $1,000, the friend — Dr. Peter Buck — offered to become Fred's partner, and a business relationship was forged that would change the landscape of the fast food industry.

The first shop was opened in Bridgeport, Connecticut in August, 1965. Then, they set a goal of having 32 stores opened in 10 years. Fred soon learned the basics of running a business, as well as the importance of serving a well-made, high quality product, providing excellent customer service, keeping operating costs low and finding great locations. These early lessons continue to serve as the foundation for successful SUBWAY restaurants around the world.[39]

It's your classic rags-to-riches story, which holds timeless appeal. I do think they have a few too many messages going on here: quality, customer service, low operating costs, and location. And the rest of the story references "quick," "nutritious," "fresh," and "delicious."

One thing I like about both the Subway and Deere stories: they have clever titles that go beyond the typical "About Us" or "Our Story." That offers readers a clue and a promise that they're about to get an actual story, and not just the usual corporate boilerplate.

PANERA

"Fast casual" restaurant chain Panera takes a completely different approach. Its history is short on humanizing details and long on financial data and corporate structure information:

The Panera Bread legacy began in 1981 as Au Bon Pain Co., Inc. ... [it] became the dominant operator within the bakery-cafe category ... between 1993 and 1997 average unit volumes increased by 75% ... In May 1999, all of Au Bon Pain Co., Inc.'s business units were sold, with the exception of Panera Bread, and the company was renamed Panera Bread ... the company's stock has grown exponentially, and today it has a market capitalization of $4.5 billion ...[40]

And so on ...

I assume Panera's target audience for this story is not customers but investors, the financial community, and potential franchisees. If so, I suppose it's a good case of knowing your audience, but I would think it leaves consumers cold.

TRADER JOE'S

Grocery chain Trader Joe's has a fun, informal take on the company history:

> *It all started in the 50s ... Would you believe we started out as a small chain of convenience stores? It's true. Way back in 1958. We were called Pronto Markets. In '67, our founder, the original Trader Joe, changed our name (yes, to Trader Joe's) and the way we do business.*
>
> *We made the stores bigger (if you can imagine), decked the walls with cedar planks and donned our crew in cool Hawaiian shirts. Most importantly, we started packaging innovative, hard-to-find, great-tasting foods under the "Trader Joe's" name. That cut our costs and saved you money. Still does. And that's important, because "Value" is a concept we take very seriously.*[41]

There's not much focus on character here, but I give them points for capturing the voice of the organization's casual, laidback brand. It's written from a first-person perspective and the tone is conversational. They even have sentence fragments! Which I'm a big fan of.

It's the perfect example of "show, don't tell," which sure beats explicitly saying, "Hey, everyone, we're the cool, casual, laidback place to shop!"

And, of course, the value proposition — value itself — is loud and clear.

I also admire the story's economy. Look at all the details they chose to *leave out* of the story: the number of stores, the locations, sales figures — even the founder's full name. Entrepreneurs aren't exactly known as shrinking violets, so that's an accomplishment in itself!

FITBIT

Newer companies face a special challenge: they don't have the rich heritage full of quaint historical details that 50- or 100-year-old organizations can mine. But fitness company FitBit makes no apologies for that and opts to keep it simple:

An Idea was Born

In 2007, our founders, Eric and James, realized that sensors and wireless technology had advanced to a point where they could bring amazing experiences to fitness and health. They embarked on a journey to create a wearable product that would change the way we move.[42]

Pretty bare bones, and closer to a positioning statement than a full-fledged story, but I give them points for simplicity and conciseness.

BONOBOS

Clothing maker Bonobos takes this approach even further:

How It All Started

We started Bonobos because we couldn't find pants that fit. They were either way too tight or too boxy. We fixed it. Now we've expanded our playbook to shirts and suits.[43]

That's it — that's the whole story. Both of these examples suggest a modern, no-nonsense approach. It's also probably no coincidence that they're both major e-commerce sites — perhaps devoted more to selling than telling.

Speaking of which ...

To Tell or Not to Tell

Still other companies don't bother at all with a history: Spirit Airlines, retailer TJ Maxx, and consultant KPMG are just a few big brands that don't have an origin story — at least on their websites.

It's possible that's meant to send a message that these businesses aren't focused on (or mired in) the past. And it's likely they tell their story in other ways, especially internally. Take ad agency Leo Burnett, for example.

LEO BURNETT

Leo Burnett is a company steeped in legend surrounding its colorful founder. You'll find little on its current website, but at every reception desk is a bowl of apples. Here's the story behind that:

> *Apples have become a symbol for the Leo Burnett Company ever since Leo Burnett put out a bowl of apples at a reception when he opened his doors in the middle of the Great Depression, which caused a lot of talk, with people saying that it would not be long before Burnett would be selling apples on the street. Apples continued*

to be a symbol of Leo Burnett's hospitality and success throughout the years.[44]

This goes to show that some of the best stories don't have to be posted on a website or framed on a boardroom wall. They live in the hearts, minds, and everyday behaviors of their employees and customers.

In the end, it comes down to audience. Who are you trying to reach, what do they need and want to know, and what's the best way to accomplish that? If you choose not to tell your story in a certain way or through a certain medium, I hope you at least have sound reasoning behind the decision.

CHAPTER 12:
HOW TO USE STORIES IN A PRESENTATION

Stories should be the centerpiece of any presentation, whether you're speaking to a small group around a conference room table or hundreds of people in a ballroom.

You should begin with story, end with story, and include stories throughout.

Here are some guidelines on how to make the most of storytelling in front of a live audience.

Start With Story

Forget everything you learned about how to kick off a presentation. Don't start by "telling them what you're going to tell them" or by walking through your agenda or explaining who you are.

Those approaches are boring. Besides, nobody cares about who you are or what you're going to say until you give them a reason to care. And you give them a reason to care by opening with a story that appeals directly to their interests.

Because you've done your homework on the audience (who they are, what they know, what they want, etc. — see Chapter 3) you can craft a story about a problem that affects them. Make sure there's an emotional component, clear conflict, high stakes, and all the other things we've talked about, and you've got them hooked.

Once hooked, they're primed for the rest of your content. Of course, that's assuming your story is actually relevant to your content, which it absolutely should be. Telling a story simply for the sake of entertaining your audience is a wasted opportunity. Storytelling should be strategic. It should reinforce your message.

Intersperse Stories Throughout (But Beware of Story Overload!)

From there, you should continue to weave stories throughout your presentation — but not too many.

I once worked with a speaking client who was a natural storyteller. He was animated, energetic, and came armed with tons of great stories. As I watched him run through his presentation I counted more than a dozen stories in the first 20 minutes. Which was about eight or ten too many.

Story overload presents several problems:

1. Audiences need variety. Too much of any one thing — even stories — is a bad idea.

2. Stories need room to breathe. By jamming them all together, the power of each one is diluted. When your stories fly by in a great big blur your audience doesn't get the time necessary to absorb and reflect on them.

3. If most of your content is stories, people will suspect that your ideas lack substance and that you, as they say in Texas, are "all hat and no cattle."

So your stories should be interspersed with data, evidence, and other "hard" content. They should act as a "palate cleanser" for the audience — a way to bring your points to life in an engaging fashion.

A Loose Guideline for Incorporating Stories

There is no hard-and-fast formula for how (and how many) stories to weave into your presentation. But that hasn't stopped people from recommending them. I've seen templates that go like this:

- Make an assertion

- Offer three pieces of evidence

- Supply data to back up the point

- Tell a story

- State the lesson

- Repeat

Like most formulas related to public speaking (and communications in general), this one is ridiculous and unworkable. Speakers aren't robots and speeches aren't flow charts.

Sometimes you might want to tee up your point by starting with a story. Or the lesson may be so self-evident that you don't need to conclude by hitting your audience over the head with it. You might even tell a story that doesn't have data or evidence to back it up. So don't feel hemmed in by a rigid structure.

Similarly, there is no set guideline for the number of stories you should tell. I usually try to have a solid story for each of the major sections of my presentation. (But not always!)

Let's say your presentation is divided into five parts: intro, conclusion, and three sections in the "body." That might call for five stories. *Might.*

It depends on many factors, including the length of the speech and the length of your stories. If you're doing a 15-minute presentation, five 2-to-3-minute stories are obviously too many. In a 40-minute speech it might be just right.

But, again, it depends. Maybe you've got several long stories or a bunch of shorter stories.

This is where instinct and the "art" comes in. If the content appears to be dragging, it might be time to add a story.

Close With Story

Because first and last impressions count for a lot, the most important parts of your presentation are the opening and close. Just as you should start with story, you should end with story. And again, it should be "on message."

If you want to really make an impact, here's a simple trick: make your closing story an extension of your opening story. Add a postscript, reveal a surprising twist, or tell it from another character's point of view.

It's like the callback that standup comics use — the ring of the familiar triggers an "aha" moment in the minds of the audience.[45] It reminds them of the journey they've been on together and gives them that satisfied feeling of having come full circle.

In a presentation I do on public speaking skills, I sometimes open with the story of the worst presenter I ever saw — someone who made every mistake in the book, from blatant self-promotion to ugly PowerPoint to talking down to us.

It's a relatable story because everyone has had to sit through an awful presentation.

It's only at the end of my talk that I reveal the kicker: the speaker that day was a professional marketer — someone whose entire career is premised on reading an audience and delivering on their needs. The point is, even people who should know better sometimes succumb to the worst presentation sins. So no one should take presenting for granted.

Try this in your next presentation and you'll see a big impact.

Now that we've covered the content — what you say — let's look at the other half of the equation: how you say it.

Tips for Delivering Your Story

Delivering a story in person involves some level of performance technique. That may sound scary to people who are uncomfortable in front of an audience, but think of it this way: it gives you the opportunity to amplify your story in a way you can't do on paper.

PRACTICE, PRACTICE, PRACTICE

First, there's no substitute for preparation. Practice your stories over and over and over again. This allows you to fine-tune them, cutting the fat so you can focus on the essentials.

It also reduces the risk of "runaway storytelling." It's very tempting when you're getting positive feedback from an audience to stretch out, embellish, and even slow down your story. Some of those ad-libs may enhance your talk, but they could just as easily kill the momentum.

STAY CONNECTED

Of course, when you've told a story dozens or hundreds of times, you run the risk of going on autopilot and sounding scripted and inauthentic.

That's where intention comes in — staying connected to your material and to your audience.

It's what great stage actors do. Night after night they perform the same show but they manage to keep it fresh and exciting for the audience. How? By staying in the moment.

Instead of simply reciting lines, they live the words and feel the ideas like it's their very first time expressing them.

So be sure to stay present. If you're describing a hot day, imagine how the sun felt on the back of your neck. If you're talking about a process, visualize the steps in your head. If you're talking about a person, picture her face.

Remember, if you check out, they will tune out.

BRING THE ENERGY

Energy is a subtle force in presenting that's hard to define. Think of it as the difference between leaning back, slumped in your seat, versus leaning forward with your elbows on the table.

It's part physical, but it also requires mental focus and emotional intensity. Quite simply, if you're not passionate about your story, why should your audience care?

To project energy, everything you do on stage should be a bit bigger than life. That means giving extra volume to your voice, expression to your face, and movement to your body.

VARY YOUR VOCAL EXPRESSION

Part of that is avoiding a quiet monotone to your vocals. Be sure to add variety by:

- "Punching up" or giving greater emphasis to key words.

- Lowering your volume at critical moments to draw the audience in and getting louder when the story calls for it.

- Speeding up as you approach the big climax and slowing down or even pausing for effect before the resolution or after a big punchline.

USE YOUR BODY TO CREATE A STAGE PICTURE

For maximum effect, get your whole body involved in telling your story: face, arms, legs — everything. That means:

- **Use your face.** Your facial expression should match your emotional intent. And that doesn't mean "acting" happy or excited or fearful or sad. Going back to the point about staying connected, you should actually be *feeling* those things in the moment, and that should be reflected in your face.

- **Use your hands.** If you're talking about your first coffee of the day, "hold" the cup in your hand. Make us see it. If you've got three points, count them off with your fingers. If you're comparing two things, gesture with your hands to one side of your body for the first thing and the other side for the second thing.

- **Mark the passage of time.** If you're taking us from past to present to future, stand at different parts of the stage to represent those phases. Also, here's a tip I learned from presentation expert Craig Hadden: as you go forward in time, move from your right to your left.[46] That way, the audience will see it as left to right, which represents the logical progression of time from their perspective.

- **Conjure your co-star.** If your story involves recreating a conversation, place that other character in a specific spot near you on stage. You can even perform both roles. That way you avoid the whole "Then I said, then he said" routine.

Bringing it All Together

Storytelling and presenting are similar in that they both require killer content and inspired delivery. And while some suggest that the performance aspect — *how* you say it — matters most, I maintain that content and delivery go hand-in-hand. Neither should be neglected.

A great performer can dazzle a crowd, but if his story is unoriginal, irrelevant to his main message, or unresponsive to the audience's needs, it's not going to have a lasting impact. On the other hand, a perfectly crafted story can be butchered by a truly inept storyteller.

They both matter. But if I had to choose, I'd err toward the content side. With a solid story, you don't necessarily need a lot of razzle-dazzle. If you practice it enough and come across as genuine and sincere, that can make up for a host of deficiencies in your presentation technique.

So don't feel like you have to be Garrison Keillor. Just be you, do your best, and make sure you believe what you're saying.

CHAPTER 13:
HOW TO TELL YOUR OWN STORY

Sometimes the hardest story to tell is the one we tell about ourselves. Modesty (false or otherwise), lack of objectivity, and insecurity all come into play.

After all, it's one thing to tell a story that bombs — the embarrassment is fleeting. But it's a whole other issue when that story is about *you*. Suddenly you're left wondering, "Did the story suck, or do *I* suck?"

The ability to tell your own story is critical to successfully navigating job interviews, networking events, and first-time meetings with others.

Here's how to prepare for the next time someone says, "So tell me about yourself."

What Not to Do: Alphabet Soup Syndrome

A few years ago I attended a meeting where the first order of business was to go around the table and take turns introducing ourselves.

It was awful. It was like an alphabet soup of job titles, company and department names, dates, dollars, and numbers:

> *I was a Quality Control Inspector for five-and-a-half years, then in 2011 I was promoted to Lead Quality Manager, then in October 2014 I transferred to the Western Region, where I was Director of Quality Assurance and managed a team of 27 inspectors and an annual budget of $42.7 million, then …*

They might as well have been reading their LinkedIn profiles aloud. It was all fact with no heart. Data with no context or meaning. In short, there was no narrative. Nothing that would stick or particularly distinguish one person from another.

Worst of all, it was boring! Imagine hearing basically the same thing, just with different data points, from 20 different people.

Turn Your Life Into a Story

That's when I realized there has to be a better way. What if we could capture the events of our careers and our lives in a form that is unique and compelling, full of conflict and drama and human interest and all the other things that make stories so effective?

Framing your career in story terms makes it more entertaining, of course, which makes people more likely to listen to and remember you. A narrative can also give context to, and help you justify, a non-traditional career path or gaps in your timeline or experience.

Finally, storytelling is a way of communicating not just *what* you do, but *why* you do it. It answers questions like:

- What sets you apart?

- What drives you?

- What do you stand for?

- What value do you offer?

- How are you making a difference?

I've worked with a lot of insurance salespeople and they're among the best storytellers I've come across. Which shouldn't be surprising since selling is about appealing to emotion, and insurance involves some pretty high-stakes drama — literally, issues of life and death.

One of my clients told this story:

I went into this business because I heard the money was good, and that's true. By the time I was 25 I was the first among my friends to own a home. But one night I got a phone call. A good friend was in a car accident and died. It was horrible, but what made it even worse was finding out that he had no plan in place to provide for his family. His wife and two young children were left with little in savings, a lot of debt, and a future of uncertainty.

For whatever reason, I had never talked to him about planning for his family's future. We were buddies, and I guess I didn't want to be one of those pushy salesmen that everybody avoids at parties. But since then I've made it my mission to help as many people as possible avoid my friend's fate. So, yes, the paycheck is nice, but for me nothing beats being able to look a customer in the eye at a time of crisis and say, "Don't worry, you're covered."

Now most of us don't deal with life-and-death matters in our everyday work. But I believe everyone has a story to tell. It may not be as dramatic as this one, but it's there, just waiting to be uncovered and shared.

Discover the Implicit Narrative of Your Career

Marketing strategist Dorie Clark talks about finding the "implicit narrative" of your life — the common thread that ties your experiences together.[47]

Whether we're aware of it or not, something is driving us forward, from job to job, experience to experience. It could be a set of values, a character trait, a skill. Even if the steps in your career path feel random and disconnected, there's often a pattern that reveals itself over time.

In a commencement address to Stanford University, Steve Jobs likened this emerging pattern to connecting the dots:

You can't connect the dots looking forward; you can only connect them looking backwards. So you have to trust that the dots will somehow connect in your future. You have to trust in something — your gut, destiny, life, karma, whatever.[48]

Creating your narrative is about connecting those dots.

Start by Examining Your Career Highlights

As a starting point, make a list of the major successes and challenges of your career and life (Clark calls them your "war stories"). Don't think too hard about it. What are the first things that come to mind — promotions, awards, rejections, failures?

Now ask yourself some questions:

- Do any themes or patterns emerge?

- What skills did you bring to bear on the problems you faced?

- What traits helped you succeed?

- What did others have to say about your role?

- What did you most enjoy about that work?

- How did it make you feel?

In creating my own story, I discovered that the thing that has driven me, satisfies me, and has been central to my success, is the desire to perform. It was there at nearly every phase of my life:

- I was the baby of the family and the natural center of attention.

- In school I was what's known as a "show-off."

- At the office I was often drafted to create Top-10 lists, sketches, and song parodies for major occasions.

- As a speechwriter, I was likely drawn to the performance aspects of the craft: the rhetorical flourishes, the emotional highs and lows, the words designed to provoke an audience reaction.

- And that all led to performing on stage, first as an actor and then as a public speaker.

Yet if you had told me years ago that I'd be standing up in front of audiences for a living, I would have thought you were insane. As Jobs said, it was impossible to predict then, but looking back, the dots were all there, ready to be connected.

Structure Your Story

To create a personal narrative, I recommend a five-part structure:

1. The beginning: the "normal state" of things.

2. Inciting incident: something that disrupts the normal state.

3. Turning point: the path you took in response.

4. Conflict: challenges along the way.

5. The end or resolution: which brings it all full circle.

To revisit our original story formula — "character, goal, challenge, resolution" — all those elements are implicit here. You, obviously, are the character, the inciting incident is the challenge, the turning point is the goal and the end is the resolution. This is just another approach that I believe works better for the personal story.

Let's apply this structure to the insurance salesman's story above:

1. In the beginning, our character is focused on a career based on financial reward.

2. The inciting incident is his friend's death.

3. That leads to the turning point: his mission to help others avoid the same mistake.

4. The conflict is his aversion to coming across as the typical insurance salesman, especially to his friends.

5. In the end, he resolves that challenge by thinking of the bigger picture: the ability to offer comfort and security to a customer in a time of need.

Think of these as guidelines, and don't worry if your particular inciting incident isn't as dramatic, or your turning point isn't as sharp. Just do the best with the experiences life has dealt you.

My Story

In fact, my own story — which I told earlier in a different form — is a little softer around the edges:

> For most of my life I pursued a conventional career in business, doing corporate communications and PR. (Beginning/normal state.) While it was satisfying and rewarding, I always felt there was something more creative calling to me. (Inciting incident.) So I scratched a long-time itch and started taking classes at Second City. (Turning point.) That grew into a second career performing on stage and in front of the camera.

For years I struggled to keep my two worlds separate. (Conflict.) I'd do my client work by day and steal away to audition and rehearse and perform at night. But the more I studied and performed, the more I realized these two worlds were not so different. They both require you to connect with audiences, to express yourself in a compelling way, and to tell stories. So I found a way to bring these two worlds together in my books and workshops. Now I'm doing the thing I love — performing on stage — while sharing the business knowledge I've accumulated. And in the process I'm helping people become more skilled, confident communicators, which is very rewarding. (Resolution.)

Now if this were a Hollywood movie the inciting incident might have been getting fired from my job for daydreaming about a show business career. And the turning point could have gone like this:

I left the office and wandered the city alone, head down in the pouring rain. I spotted a reflection in a puddle and looked up — it was the warm glow of the Second City marquee. Like a beacon, it drew me inside, where I discovered the welcoming embrace of a group of like-minded creatives. I was home!

But that's not how it went. There were multiple possible inciting incidents and turning points over a period of years, most of which would take too long to cover and detract from the point of the story.

Again, storytelling is about making choices — and those choices are driven by our goals, the audience, and, in the case of a personal story, our own comfort level with revealing the details of our lives.

Remember Your Audience

Which brings up another important point: as with any other communication, your personal story needs to be finely tuned to your audience's interests and needs. If you're in a job interview, what set of qualities is the hiring manager looking for? If you're selling, what is the buyer interested in?

So you may have slightly different versions of your story — or even completely different stories — for different occasions and audiences. If I'm talking to a potential corporate consulting client, I might downplay the speaking career and emphasize instead how my acting training has made me a more creative partner in helping companies and individuals communicate successfully.

Keep Working at It

Developing your personal narrative may not come naturally at first. If you're having trouble, try getting input from people who know you well.

Depending on the circumstances, it may useful to bring in elements from your personal life — a cross-country trip that opened your eyes, an illness that lent perspective, a friend who left a mark on you. In fact, mining your personal experience may be necessary if you're at an early point in your career.

To sharpen your narrative, go back to the tips in Chapter 2 on story structure and Chapter 6 on focusing your story. Don't neglect the emotional component discussed in Chapter 4. That's what will make you more relatable.

Remember: the point is not to capture every twist and turn of your life or career. The goal is to give people a glimpse of who you are and pique their interest enough that they'll want to know more.

CHAPTER: 14:
HOW TO TELL YOUR PERSONAL BRAND STORY

In a Facebook post a while back I raised the issue of having a "personal brand," to which a friend responded, "Barf." I know she's not alone in her thinking.

After all, we are not dish soap ("cuts through grease!") or paper towels ("the quicker picker upper!").

So if the term makes you queasy, think of your brand as your reputation. You'd consider that important, right?

Why Brand Yourself?

Your personal brand can be a practical tool that helps set you apart in the workplace and the marketplace. It can help you land the right job, earn a raise or promotion, and get the recognition you deserve. It can also make you a more credible and effective champion on behalf of your company, cause, or team.

Capturing your brand in the form of a story allows you to promote yourself in a way that feels natural, comfortable, and not overly ... well, promotional.

Do it right and your brand can even help you manage your priorities better, adding a little more sanity to your life.

Finally, your brand can help guide you through a crisis. Storytelling expert Bernadette Jiwa emphasizes aligning your behaviors with your brand story. When the unexpected happens, you may not know exactly *what* to do, but a well-defined brand can guide you in *how* you behave. She recommends asking questions like, "Does this represent what we stand for?" and "Does this feel like us?"[49]

What is a Personal Brand?

Over the years, I've sat through more than my share of corporate branding presentations. I confess that half the time I have no idea what they're talking about. The other half of the time I suspect *they* don't know what they're talking about.

But from what I've gathered, it doesn't have to be overly complicated. Your brand is essentially what you're known for — the unique combination of qualities you bring to the table that make people want to work or do business with you.

Importantly, your brand *will* happen, whether you know it or not and whether you like it or not. In the words of Bonnie Gillespie, who teaches actors how to market themselves, "You're building your brand daily, either by design or by default."[50]

So you could be branded a difficult person or a scatterbrain or a basic hot mess. Wouldn't you rather try to define it yourself? I know I would.

We Can Only Control so Much

But that's the catch. Your brand isn't what *you* say it is, it's what *others* say it is. Just because you brand yourself a creative genius doesn't automatically make it so. You have to be viewed by others that way.

So some of this is beyond your control. You can't change who you are by slapping a label on yourself.

But you can start to affect people's perceptions by carefully thinking about your brand, communicating it, and acting on it.

It's all about taking charge of your story.

How to Figure Out Your Brand

Since your brand isn't simply what *you* want it to be, it's important to turn your gaze outward.

Returning to what we discussed in the last chapter, think about the challenges you've faced in your career and your life. What specific skills and traits were instrumental to overcoming those challenges?

Here are a few other ways to get at this information:

- Think about the times people bring you onto a team at work. What are they generally looking for from you? What role do you end up playing?

- Look at your past performance reviews. What themes emerge?

- What about awards, honors, and accolades? Are there any patterns there?

Ideally, the information from these sources should be consistent with how you position yourself on your resume, LinkedIn, company bio, and other places where you describe yourself.

If they're not consistent, you have some work to do, either in how you position yourself or in how you conduct yourself. Believe me, the former is much easier to fix than the latter!

Examples of Personal Brands

So what do you see? Are you:

- **The Analyzer** — the one who thinks through every angle of a problem?

- **The Organizer** — who puts all the pieces together and harnesses the right resources?

- **The Innovator** — the person who comes up with the bright idea?

- **The Cool Cucumber** — the proverbial calm at the center of the storm?

- **The Bulldog** — the tenacious fighter who breaks through all the obstacles?

Those are just a few examples to spur your thinking.

How to Present Your Brand to the World

Your brand will be represented in ways both superficial and substantive. Superficial is less important, but it's more fun, so let's start with that!

On the surface, your brand might be reflected in how you present yourself to the world, from the way you dress to the appearance of your workspace. If you're the Innovator, you will probably dress in a modern or unconventional way. If you're the Organizer, a desk that's buried in paper will surely undermine your brand. (And may be an indication that that's *not* your brand.)

While appearances count, they should not represent the majority of your brand focus. If you do it right, your brand will actually guide your behavior:

- If you have the luxury of choosing your assignments at work, your brand should influence which projects you take on. After all, your brand represents your strengths. If you're an analytical person and do your best work locked away in a windowless room breaking down a problem, you're probably not the ideal choice to send on a customer-schmoozing mission.

- Outside of work you have more control over your agenda, so your brand might drive the kinds of activities you get involved with in your community. This is not about being selfish; it's about playing to your strengths and helping out in the best way you can. If you want to help with the school fundraiser and you're lousy with money, don't sign up to be treasurer!

- Your brand will also affect how and what you communicate, from the way you describe yourself in writing to how you introduce yourself, to what you choose to contribute in meetings. All of that should be "on-brand."

The implication here is that a successful brand requires discipline and the ability to say "no" to those things that are not in your area of expertise.

On the positive side, the things you say "yes" to will reinforce your brand, creating a virtuous cycle: the more you become known for certain things, the more you will be sought out for (and get to do) those things.

And that should result in greater satisfaction and peace of mind.

The Role of Your Brand Story

Once you have your brand figured out, you should work to capture it in a story. Here are some of the occasions that might call for a brand story:

- In job interviews, when you're asked about your greatest strengths.

- On sales calls, when prospects want to know why they should choose you over your competitors.

- When you're introducing yourself to a new group of people and you want to communicate who you are.

Your brand story should be structured like any other story — character (you), goal, challenge, resolution. For the source of your stories, mine your experience. Think about:

- Major work/career accomplishments

- Awards you've won

- How you solved a problem

- Why you do what you do

- Why you joined the organization you're now working for

- Why you started your business

Examples of Brand Stories

Here are a few examples of how a brand story can play out:

- *I'm the kind of person who just can't let go of a problem. My co-workers know this. We'll be in a meeting discussing a bunch of issues and we'll hit a roadblock. After some debate we'll agree to table the issue and come back to it later. But they say I get this look on my face, and they know I'm not done with it. And I'm not. I will mull it over, stew on it, obsess over it, night and day, until I finally figure out an approach. It's just the way I'm wired.*

- *A long-time customer told me that I'm the least "salesy" salesperson he's ever worked with. When I drop by his office I don't go in with a planned pitch. We'll talk about his business and whatever problem he's dealing with at the time. If I can help solve it, I do — even if it has nothing to do with one of our products. That approach seems to work. He's been my #1 customer for 15 years.*

- *I sometimes find the less I know about an issue the better. I'll drop into a meeting where a task force has been working on a problem for weeks, grinding away, trying to figure out a solution. Then I'll ask what feels like a really stupid question but it leads to an "aha" moment that produces a breakthrough. They were just stuck in a groove and it took a fresh perspective for them to break out of it. So that's what I do around here — I ask the weird questions nobody thought to ask and help people get unstuck.*

One thing these stories have in common is an undercurrent of humility, which is important if you don't want to alienate your audience. So how do you talk about yourself without sounding like you're totally full of yourself?

How to Talk About Yourself Without Sounding Like a Jerk

It starts with positioning. Try playing the role of the unexpected or accidental hero. If everyone around you is losing their head and you enter the room in an aura of light to rescue them from their ignorance ... then, yeah, you're going to sound like a jerk.

Instead, frame it more modestly: "None of us knew what to do, then an idea occurred to me. I didn't know whether it would work but we all agreed it was worth a try ..."

Your tone and expression are important, too. You should not only come across as sincere and authentic, you should actually *be* sincere and authentic.

Authenticity produces credibility. Your audience is much more likely to *believe* you if they believe *in* you.

Another option is to attribute your stories to others: "Here's what one of my oldest customers had to say ..." or "This is what I hear most often from my co-workers ..."

Now there are some people — a rare few — who can brag about themselves in a way that's utterly charming. Muhammad Ali comes to mind. Beyond him, I can't think of many other examples — so for most of us mortals a little humility is called for.

Not that you should undersell yourself either. A big part of professional development is coming to a clear understanding of your strengths and your weaknesses and being able to communicate both without apology.

It's a fine line. Most reasonably self-aware people will know where it's drawn. Or, by sensing the reactions of their listeners, will at least be able to figure out when they've crossed it.

Give it Time

If you're early in your career, you may have trouble defining your brand. Be patient and keep at it. Draw on your education and life experience. Try asking others for their input.

Once you've nailed your brand and can sustain it through your communication and behavior, you'll be better able to stand out from the crowd and help people recognize your value.

And don't feel hemmed in — just as you grow and evolve or take different directions in your career, your brand can develop and change over time.

Just remember: *you* have to be the one steering the ship. If you don't take control of defining and articulating your brand, it will be defined for you!

CHAPTER 15:
HOW TO USE STORY
FOR A TOAST, TRIBUTE,
OR EULOGY

There comes a time in everyone's life where we are asked to "say a few words" on a special occasion, give a toast to the happy couple, or deliver the eulogy for a loved one.

There's a lot of pressure in these situations. You want to do justice to the honoree and say something meaningful. You worry about disappointing the crowd. And you may be overcome with emotion. None of which helps you focus.

So you end up delivering a laundry list of superlatives — so-and-so is (or was) kind, considerate, generous, funny, witty, gregarious, adventurous, free-spirited, hard-working, principled, loyal, humble, courageous, and so on ...

That's where story comes in. A story can help you frame and focus your thoughts. It may even be easier to deliver. And, of course, stories pack unparalleled power to move people.

A Lesson from Paul McCartney

Paul McCartney is one of the great storytellers of all time. When Beatles producer George Martin died, McCartney penned a concise and evocative tribute that serves as an excellent model for how it's done.[51]

First, he started with three simple descriptors, calling Martin "the most generous, intelligent and musical person" he had ever known. You can't go wrong with the classic "rule of threes."

Note also that these adjectives are specific, as opposed to words like amazing, wonderful, fantastic, and their ilk.

Speaking of specificity, McCartney offers "proof" of these traits by saying Martin was "like a second father" and truly "the fifth Beatle."

Then Sir Paul tells a story to illustrate Martin's musical knowledge, explaining how the producer urged McCartney to add a string quartet to the song "Yesterday," and walked him through the process of creating the arrangement. McCartney credits Martin for the song's success.

Importantly, he doesn't tell two or three or five stories — just as he wouldn't put several different choruses in one song. That's discipline.

Finally, after extolling Martin's musical genius, McCartney provides a nice counterpoint by noting that the producer was humble and self-effacing "[e]ven when he was Knighted by the Queen."

The First Rule: There are No Rules

Delivering a tribute or eulogy is obviously highly personal, so I would never recommend an iron-clad template or set of rules.

However, the most popular blog post I've ever written was on how to write a eulogy, so it's clear that people are seeking guidance.[52] My rule then was to ignore all the so-called rules.

But as the page visits piled up, I felt compelled to offer a little more structure in the form of 10 tips.[53]

Here I've consolidated some of my best advice.

Guidelines for Composing a Tribute or Eulogy

- First and foremost, **speak from the heart.** If a particular memory or observation is meaningful to you, it will probably be meaningful to others.

- **Avoid the laundry list.** Try to narrow your loved one's many outstanding qualities to a few. Three is the magic number, but I wouldn't fault you if you chose two or four.

- **Pick one quality to focus on.** From your list, choose one quality and make that your "theme."

- **Compose a story.** Find a story that exemplifies that quality. It could be a big event, like a major life turning point, or some small moment. It can even be a funny story. A little comic relief is welcome at times like these.

- **Attend to the small details.** Don't forget the small sensory details that give a story more impact. If I was telling a story about my grandfather, I might mention the call of the mourning doves that were always in the backyard, or the smell of sawdust in his wood shop, or the steaks sizzling on the giant brick barbecue he built.

- **Cut the excess details.** Don't let the extraneous details weigh your story down. (See Chapter 6.)

- **Draw a lesson.** Can you bring the story back to how it had an impact on you or others? Something you learned or how you might live your life differently as a result?

- **Use a quote.** A quote that captures the point you're making can be a great way to introduce or conclude your message. People love quotes and an online search will turn up plenty of options on almost any subject. You can make it personal by choosing a work of literature, film, or a biblical passage that's meaningful to you or your loved one.

- **Mind the clock.** There are no hard-and-fast rules for how long you should speak. A toast is generally shorter than a eulogy. Remember, people are at a party and drinking, so attention spans are short! A eulogy might run several minutes or longer — it depends on whether others are speaking and your own ability to get through it. Consult with whoever's officiating for guidance.

How to Deliver a Eulogy or Toast

Now comes the hard part: getting through what will likely be a deeply emotional moment. This can be particularly challenging for people who aren't comfortable emoting in public. Here are some tips:

- **Practice.** As with a business presentation, you should practice, practice, practice. My father's death was a long time coming, and I spent months thinking about what he meant to me and what I might tell others about him. You may not have that "luxury," but make the most of whatever time you have.

- **Notes are okay.** There's no shame in using notes or a script. Even if you don't read off of them, they're a comfort to have in case you lose focus, which is easy to do when emotions are running high.

- **Expect the unexpected.** You can never predict how you will react in the moment. There were parts of my father's eulogy that I thought I'd never get through, but they sailed right by.[54] And yet a single, seemingly innocuous detail unexpectedly struck a chord and caused me to choke up. You just never know.

- **Don't over-apologize.** If you lose your composure, start to cry, or stumble over the words, try not to worry about it. Believe me, nobody's judging you for having feelings. If you want to say, "I'm sorry," that's fine, but there's no need to go on and on with the apologies. People understand.

- **Pause and breathe.** To regain your composure, just pause and take a few breaths. (In fact, make sure you're breathing deeply throughout — it's incredibly important for centering yourself.[55])

- **Humor works.** In a eulogy, people will appreciate some comic relief. In a wedding or other toast, be careful. Don't be the person who tells inappropriate or inside jokes that make the honorees and the crowd squirm. It's a tribute, not a roast. And I hope it goes without saying that you should stay sober — at least until you've finished the job!

- **Be careful with eye contact.** Normally I advise speakers to make eye contact with audience members. Focusing on the friendly face of a loved one in a difficult moment may provide comfort. On the other hand, it could completely break you and reduce you to tears. So if you're uncertain, this is one instance where I'd say it's okay to minimize eye contact.

Most of all, forgive yourself. Especially at a funeral, you're not going to be in the ideal state of mind. Don't worry about making it perfect, don't worry about pleasing the people there, don't worry about the deceased looking down on you in judgment. Just do your best and let the rest go.

What if Your Relationship with the Person is "Complicated"?

Years ago I worked with a "difficult" person. He was a terrible manager and bad for morale, leaving chaos and frustrated employees in his wake. One day in our usual weekly staff meeting he announced he was leaving the company (under circumstances left deliberately vague, as often happens in these instances).

The relief in the room was palpable. But then people around the table started offering up spontaneous glowing tributes: "I'll miss you." NOT! "You were a great manager." WRONG! "I really enjoyed working with you." LIE!

I was appalled. To me it's an issue of integrity. You say what you mean and mean what you say. But a lot of people will reflexively default to platitudes in times like these because it seems like the nice thing to do.

But let's say you're like me and paying phony tribute to someone you don't particularly like goes against your principles. What to do?

A Lesson from Acting

Here's where my acting training comes in. Sometimes you're cast in a role with someone who's supposed to be your best buddy or love interest and for whatever reason, the two of you do not click. It's simply not a person you would enjoy spending time with in real life.

When this happens, you work to find something — and maybe it's just *one* thing — that's admirable about this person. If you believe as I do that everyone has something of value to offer, it shouldn't be that hard.

So in the case of our departing colleague, you might say, "I've always admired your tenacity" or even, "I'll never forget your laugh." Or you can keep it neutral and ambiguous, with something like, "This place sure won't be the same without you!"

Tell the Truth (to an Extent)

For a eulogy, your job will be a little harder. I think it's okay to be honest (if not brutally so). Nobody expects a person to be perfect or a relationship to be free of discord. Perhaps you acknowledge it obliquely, or make a small joke about it.

From there you pivot to something positive — "He always tried hard" or "She did her best with what she had."

To the extent possible, this is a time to practice a little forgiveness.

The Beauty of Story

And here's where story can save you. A story frees you from having to lavish empty praise. It simply recounts an experience without necessarily committing you to a specific judgment about that experience.

You could even solicit other people's stories and act as a "reporter" of sorts. That way you don't have to compromise your integrity.

That's the beauty of storytelling. It's not just an important way to connect; in some cases it offers welcome detachment.

CONCLUSION:
STAND UP, STAND OUT

I often wrap up my storytelling workshops with a story about comic actor and writer Ricky Gervais:

> *Years ago, Ricky Gervais had a crazy idea for a new workplace comedy. It would be a mash-up of the traditional sitcom and reality TV, complete with shaky hand-held camerawork and characters breaking the "fourth wall" to talk directly to viewers.*
>
> *And at its center was the squirm-inducing David Brent, an insufferable jerk hardly cut from the cloth of likable workplace characters such as Mary Tyler Moore or Liz Lemon.*
>
> *But Gervais pitched his idea to the BBC, it got the green light, and "The Office" went on to become one of the most successful shows in television history.*
>
> *How did it happen?*
>
> *According to a BBC executive who was there that day, it wasn't so much what Gervais said in the meeting, but how he said it. He was so committed, so enthusiastic — he believed so much in the idea — that the executives couldn't help believe in it, too.*

I tell this story because it illustrates so many important lessons about the craft of storytelling.

Structure it Tightly

First, the story follows a simple structure. Our character is Ricky Gervais, his goal is to get his show produced, and the challenge or obstacle he faces is that it's a radical concept for an industry that usually goes with the safe bet.

He resolves this challenge by bowling the executives over with his passion and belief in the project.

Not every story has to follow this structure — there are endless alternatives out there. Find one that works for you. But do make sure there's clear conflict and stakes and a character that people can relate to. Or in this case, since Gervais is not everyone's cup of tea, a problem or goal people can relate to, like the pursuit of a dream.

Focus on the Essentials

There's a lot more detail I could have added to this story. For instance, Gervais was accompanied on that pitch by his creative partner Stephen Merchant. But that adds a second character who's not as familiar to most people.

I'd either have to explain who he is or leave the audience wondering, "Stephen Merchant, Stephen Merchant … do I know that name? Where have I seen him?" By that time they've missed some core elements of the story.

I also omitted minor details like the date and year of the pitch meeting and the name and title of the BBC executive.

Would identifying him as "Jon Plowman, BBC's Head of Comedy Entertainment" significantly add to the story? Probably to Mr. Plowman, but not to the rest of us.

And there were some fun and interesting details as well. According to Gervais, he told the executives, "It's either me in it, writing and directing, or not at all," to which Merchant replied (after the meeting), "Can I do the talking in the future?"

That's pretty funny, but not quite on point, and thus potentially distracting.

Finally, I paraphrased the producer's words. Here's what he actually said:

> *In their heads it was already a hit in Britain and a hit in the U.S., and they were absolutely certain about it. And that sort of thing is infectious, and you think, Well, hooray — if they believe it, then I'll believe it. And maybe the actors will believe it, and maybe the viewers will believe it eventually.*

Storytelling is about condensing and interpreting events in order to better ensure audience understanding.

Tailor Your Story for Audience and Goal

Stories should always be fine-tuned to the audience and consistent with our goals.

For instance, if I were telling this story to an insider crowd, like TV people, the details about Merchant and Plowman might resonate with them. Similarly, I might use more industry jargon or shorthand for this group.

Also, there are multiple lessons that could be the focus of the story, from believing in yourself to taking risks to exhibiting passion. It all depends on the message being communicated.

Always be Looking for Stories

How did I find this story? It wasn't through a Google search, and it wasn't handed to me via a clickbait-style article headlined "10 Things Ricky Gervais Can Teach Us About Passion in the Workplace."

I found it because I happened to be reading a *New York Times Magazine* feature on Gervais.[56] Buried within that 3,500-word article were two paragraphs that got my attention and became the basis for this story.

Always be on the lookout for great stories, whether you're reading, watching TV, playing with your children or pets, sitting in traffic, or doing the grocery shopping. Stories are everywhere, just waiting to be discovered.

Be Original

An original story has two advantages: 1) you have the opportunity to make it your own; and 2) people haven't heard it before.

Now the Gervais story isn't exactly original. It was told by Gervais himself, then retold by the *Times* reporter. But it's not a story that's widely known and I've put it in a form and context that's fairly different from the original.

So a story that you find on your own and interpret in your way is far different from, say, the starfish story from Chapter

8, which has appeared on countless posters, needlepoints, and Internet memes.

I create other lesser-known stories from episodes of "Star Trek," movies like *The Fugitive*, and books, magazines and other reading. It sure beats being the 100 millionth person to relate the *bon mot* about Winston Churchill telling off the lady who criticized his drinking.[57]

Bring the Passion

Finally, the Gervais story is about passion, and passion sells. It's essential to storytelling and it's part of what makes people like and want to do business with us.

If you can find and tell stories that are meaningful to you, either because you experienced them personally or they speak to values you hold dear, you'll make a bigger impact and have greater influence on those around you.

Stand Up, Stand Out

That, ultimately, is the true power of storytelling. Our stories help define who we are and what we stand for. They set us apart in a noisy, competitive world. And they help ensure we're remembered.

Don't be intimidated. Storytelling isn't reserved for artists and poets and folksy cowboys huddled around the campfire. It's a practical tool anyone can use to get their point across.

It doesn't have to be complicated. Three simple elements — character, goal, challenge — are all you need to get started. (And if you happen to like it complicated, there are plenty of experts out there who will take you through their 20-step storytelling process!)

Most of all, don't hold back. Don't let fear override your desire to share. Be open and generous and allow your individuality to shine through.

That is the key to creating authentic connections, strengthening your relationships, and getting more of what you want out of your work and your life.

ENDNOTES

Introduction: Why Storytelling is Essential to Success

1. Jennifer Aaker, "Persuasion and the Power of Story," YouTube (September 14, 2013).

Chapter 1: What Makes Stories So Powerful?

2. "Average daily TV viewing time per person in selected countries worldwide in 2015," Statista (2017).

3. Kendall Haven, *Story Proof: The Science Behind the Startling Power of Story* (Libraries Unlimited: 2007).

4. Leo Widrich, "The Science of Storytelling: Why Telling a Story is the Most Powerful Way to Activate Our Brains," Lifehacker (December 5, 2012).

5. Paul J. Zak, "Why Your Brain Loves Good Storytelling," *Harvard Business Review* (October 28, 2014).

6. Annie Murphy Paul, "Your Brain on Fiction," *New York Times* (March 17, 2012).

7. Nancy Duarte, "The Secret Structure of Great Talks," TED.com (November 2011).

8. Chip and Dan Heath, *Made to Stick: Why Some Ideas Survive and Others Die*, (Random House: 2007).

9. Nick Collins, "Brain Wired to Remember Emotionally Charged Events," *The Telegraph* (August 23, 2012).

Chapter 2: What is a Story?

10. Michael Neelsen, "Storytelling Tip: The Principle of 'Buts' and 'Therefores'," Story First Media.

11. Jim Camp, "Decisions Are Emotional, Not Logical: the Neuroscience Behind Decision Making," Big Think.

Chapter 4: Emotion Fuels Stories

12. Antonio Damasio, *Descartes' Error: Emotion, Reason, and the Human Brain* (Penguin Books: 2005).

13. Drake Baer, "How Only Being Able to Use Logic to Make Decisions Destroyed a Man's Life," *New York Magazine* [n.d.]

14. James B. Stewart, "When Cars Meet Politics, A Clash," *New York Times* (February 10, 2012).

15. Chrysler, "It's Halftime in America," YouTube (February 7, 2012).

16. Chris O'Brien, "Apple's Tim Cook Gets Feisty, Funny and Fiery at Shareholders Meeting," *Los Angeles Times* (March 1, 2014).

17. Simon Sinek, *Start with Why: How Great Leaders Inspire Everyone to Take Action* (Portfolio: 2011).

Chapter 6: How to Focus Your Story

18. The Simpsons, "Last Exit to Springfield," IMDB, quotes.

19. Jessica Strawser, "Writing Advice from Stephen King & Jerry Jenkins," Writer's Digest (July 21, 2009).

20. Matthew Dicks, "Four Essential Lies," as told to Mike Pesca, host of Slate's "The Gist" podcast (June 22, 2015).

Chapter 7: How to Preserve the Integrity of Your Stories

21. Deloitte, "A Day Like Any Other," YouTube (May 11, 2015).

Chapter 8: How and Where to Find Great Stories

22. Steven Covey, "The Big Rocks of Life," appleseeds.org.

23. "Lighthouse and Naval Vessel Urban Legend," Wikipedia.

24. Joel Barker, "The Star Thrower Story," starthrower.com.

25. "Nova Don't Go," Snopes (March 19, 2011).

Chapter 9: Story's Cousins: Comparison, Analogy, and Metaphor

26. Jonah Berger, "Why 'Cool' is Still Cool," *New York Times* (November 20, 2015).

27. Paul Gillin, "Create Stuff They've Just Gotta Read: How to Write for Social Networks," SlideShare (November 12, 2015).

28. Anthony Doerr, *All the Light We Cannot See: A Novel* (Scribner: 2014).

29. Douglas van Praet, "Why Metaphors Beat The Snot Out Of Facts When It Comes To Motivating Action," *Fast Company* (July 29, 2015).

30. John F. Kennedy, "Moon Speech — Rice Stadium," nasa.gov.

Chapter 10: The Dark Side of Storytelling

31. Sam Wang and Sandra Aamodt, "Your Brain Lies to You," *New York Times* (June 29, 2008).

32. Rachel Weiner, "Mitt Romney Blimp Crash Lands in Florida," *Washington Post* (October 22, 2012).

33. Brendan Nyhan, "The Momentum Behind a Misleading Narrative," *Columbia Journalism Review* (October 22, 2012).

34. Lauren Carroll, "Timeline of Brian Williams' Statements on Iraqi Helicopter Attack," Punditfact (February 5, 2015).

35. Sam Wang, "Your Brain Lies to You" (June 29, 2008).

36. James McGaugh, quoted by Erika Hyasaki, "How Many of Our Memories Are Fake?," *The Atlantic* (November 18, 2013).

37. Alison George, "I Could Have Sworn … Why You Can't Trust Your Memory," New Scientist (August 21, 2013).

Chapter 11: How to Tell Your Company's Origin Story

38. "The Plow That Started it All," deere.com, Our Company>History.

39. "The Seventeen-Year-Old Entrepreneur," subway.com, About Us>History.

40. "Our History," panerabread.com, Our Company>About Panera Bread>History of the Company.

41. "Our Story," traderjoes.com, Our Story.

42. "An Idea Was Born," fitbit.com, About Us.

43. "How it All Started," bonobos.com, About Us.

44. "Leo Burnett: Apples," Wikipedia.

Chapter 12: How to Use Stories in a Presentation

45. "Callback (comedy)," Wikipedia.

46. I received this advice directly from Craig Hadden. More great tips can be found on his blog, "Remote Possibilities," on WordPress.

Chapter 13: How to Tell Your Own Story

47. Dorie Clark, "Discover Your Personal Narrative," *Harvard Business Review* (June 28, 2013).

48. "Steve Jobs Stanford Commencement Speech 2005," YouTube.

Chapter 14: How to Tell Your Personal Brand Story

49. Bernadette Jiwa, "How to Stay True to Your Brand Story," The Story of Telling blog.

50. "You're Building Your Brand Daily ...," via Pinterest. While Bonnie Gillespie's marketing advice is targeted to actors, I find many of the strategies she teaches can apply to those looking to advance their career in practically any field. See bonniegillespie.com.

Chapter 15: How to Use Story for a Toast, Tribute, or Eulogy

51. "Paul McCartney on George Martin," paulmccartney.com (March 9, 2016).

52. Rob Biesenbach, "How to Write a Eulogy: Lessons from My Dad's Funeral," robbiesenbach.com (September 10, 2013).

53. Rob Biesenbach, "How to Write a Eulogy and Deliver It: 10 Tips," robbiesenbach.com (October 30, 2013).

54. Rob Biesenbach, "Eulogy for My Father," robbiesenbach.com (September 19, 2012).

55. Stew Smith, "The Importance of Breathing," military.com.

Conclusion: Stand Up, Stand Out

56. Dave Itzkoff, "Ricky Gervais Would Like to Nonapologize," *The New York Times Magazine* (January 11, 2012.)

57. Richard M. Langworth, "Drunk and Ugly: The Rumor Mill," winstonchurchill.org.

ACKNOWLEDGMENTS

Writing a book the same year my wife and I welcomed a new baby to the family may be the craziest thing I've ever tried — and I've jumped out of an airplane.

It could not have happened without a lot of help. First, I am grateful to the stellar clients I've had the privilege to work with over the years. They've been a rich source of stories that I got to witness and experience first-hand — so I've rarely had to Google for the examples you see in this book.

Second, I've enjoyed the services of a talented team of experts, including Jane Dixon-Smith, of JD Smith-Design, who created the cover and designed the interior; Liz Dexter at LibroEditing, who copyedited the manuscript; and Pam Tierney, who produced the audio book. Hire them. If they can put up with my persnicketiness, they can handle anyone.

Finally, I am eternally grateful to Karen, who did most of the figurative and literal heavy lifting in those first few months of our new baby's life.

ABOUT THE AUTHOR

 Rob Biesenbach is an award-winning consultant who helps Fortune 500 companies and executives communicate with more purpose, power and impact. An in-demand speaker and trainer, he has delivered programs for clients including AARP, Allstate, Big Brothers Big Sisters, Deloitte, and Lockheed Martin.

Rob is a former vice president at Ogilvy PR Worldwide, where he co-founded the global employee communications practice. He was also press secretary to a state attorney general and a nonprofit and association executive in Washington, DC.

As a Second City-trained actor and improviser, he has appeared in nearly 200 stage and commercial productions, including major campaigns for BMO Harris, Blue Cross Blue Shield, ScottTrade, and Walgreens. Although he's not a doctor, he's played one on TV.

Rob lives just outside Chicago in scenic Evanston, Illinois with his wife, two enchanting children and, as of this writing, no dogs.

ALSO BY ROB BIESENBACH

ACT LIKE YOU MEAN BUSINESS

Act Like You Mean Business: Essential Communication Lessons from Stage and Screen applies the best lessons from show business to help you succeed in your business.

You'll learn how to better connect with audiences, express your ideas more creatively, write more vividly and concisely, improve your listening skills, use humor safely and effectively, and a wealth of other vital lessons.

You'll come away with practical tips you can use every day to communicate more successfully, whether you're giving a presentation, sending an email, running a meeting, closing a sale, or interviewing for a job.

Act Like You Mean Business was published in 2011 by Brigantine Media and is available in paperback and ebook from Amazon.

11 DEADLY PRESENTATION SINS

11 Deadly Presentation Sins: A Path to Redemption for Public Speakers, PowerPoint Users, and Anyone Who Has to Get Up and Talk in Front of an Audience, is a fun, practical guide packed with more than 100 indispensable tips you can use right away to deliver a more powerful presentation.

You'll learn how to open with a bang instead of a whimper, focus and structure your content, create more compelling visuals, make the most of body language, and bring energy to your delivery, among other important skills.

Whether you're talking to colleagues, customers or the community, in a boardroom, ballroom, or church basement, you'll come away with the confidence and skills you need when all eyes are on you.

11 Deadly Presentation Sins was published in 2014 and is available in paperback, ebook and audiobook (narrated by the author) from Amazon, Barnes & Noble, Kobo, iBooks, and iTunes.

JOIN ME FOR MORE VALUABLE TIPS

If you enjoyed this book and want to continue the journey toward becoming a more powerful and persuasive communicator, I invite you to join my email list. Every month you'll get practical tips from me as well as the best thinking from experts I follow.

Here are a few of the subjects I've covered:

- The Tina Fey Guide to Success in the Workplace

- Do you Suffer from Resting (Skeptical) Face? 3 Quick Cures

- How to Say No and Preserve Your Sanity

- 10 Steps for Cutting the Fat From Your Writing

- How to Get Along With Others: 3 Acting Tricks That Really Work

- 5 Critical Things to Do Right Before a Presentation

- How to Deliver a Real Apology

If that sounds interesting, follow this link: www.RobBiesenbach.com/joinme

Or go to my website, www.RobBiesenbach.com, and enter your email address in the form near the bottom of the home page. You'll also get bonus materials to help transform the way you communicate.

CPSIA information can be obtained
at www.ICGtesting.com
Printed in the USA
LVHW011737040820
662391LV00013B/1194